CAIRN

BOOKS BY PEGGY SHUMAKER

Poetry

Toucan Nest

Gnawed Bones

Greatest Hits (chapbook)

Blaze (a collaboration with painter Kesler Woodward)

Underground Rivers

Wings Moist from the Other World

Braided River (letterpress chapbook)

The Circle of Totems

Esperanza's Hair

Lyrical Memoir

Just Breathe Normally

CAIRN

new and selected poems and prose by

PEGGY SHUMAKER

with an introduduction by

KEVIN CLARK

Red Hen Press | *Pasadena, CA*

Cairn: New and Selected Poems and Prose

Book design by Selena Trager

Library of Congress Cataloging-in-Publication Data
Names: Shumaker, Peggy, 1952–author.
Title: Cairn: new and selected poems and prose / Peggy Shumaker.
Other titles: Poems. Selections
Description: Pasadena, California: Red Hen Press, [2018] | Includes bibliographical references.
Identifiers: LCCN 2017034739 | ISBN 9781597096119| eISBN 9781597096935
Classification: LCC PS3569.H778 A6 2018 | DDC 811/.54—dc23
LC record available at https://lccn.loc.gov/2017034739

The National Endowment for the Arts, the Los Angeles County Arts Commission, the Ahmanson Foundation, the Dwight Stuart Youth Fund, the Max Factor Family Foundation, the Pasadena Tournament of Roses Foundation, the Pasadena Arts & Culture Commission and the City of Pasadena Cultural Affairs Division, the City of Los Angeles Department of Cultural Affairs, the Audrey & Sydney Irmas Charitable Foundation, the Kinder Morgan Foundation, the Allergan Foundation, the Riordan Foundation, and the Amazon Literary Partnership partially support Red Hen Press.

First Edition
Published by Red Hen Press
www.redhen.org

for my family by blood and by choice

for my students, who continue to teach me

&

for my beloved Joe

CONTENTS

New Poems

Placing Our Feet with Care on This Earth

Sparks

a conversation in poems and paintings

Impossible Grace

from Esperanza's Hair

from The Circle of Totems

from Wings Moist from the Other World

from Underground Rivers

from Blaze

from Gnawed Bones

from Toucan Nest

from Just Breathe Normally

CAIRN

INTRODUCTION

Peggy Shumaker is a discreet radical. Her poems are paradoxically marked by sonic restraint, thus augmenting her radically expansive belief in emotional freedom. She exhibits a resolve to push against long-held, surely patriarchal ideas about the boundaries of sentiment. Holding to a notion of reality not unlike Federico Garcia Lorca's duende, she realizes that perception is a constantly reforming, even dreamlike, journey. She's not limited by compulsory notions of reserved expression that have marked so much English language poetry, especially since T. S. Eliot's "doctrine of impersonality" (1919) came to mean that emotion was not to be trusted. Dylan Thomas, Sylvia Plath, and perhaps a few of the Beats may have briefly broken from traditional tonal constraint, but over the last century most poets have felt safe within a threnodic voice that resists poles of joy and grief and love.

Shumaker's breakthrough poetry doesn't reject threnody, that dreamlike tone of lamentation we've heard throughout the history of verse, but her poetry nonetheless goes far beyond old-fashioned mourning songs. Over time her poems come to assert a new understanding: that Eliot's post-Romantic conception of poetic voice is circumscribed by an unrealistically thin band of expression, one that keeps poets from exploring the full spectrum of human feeling. Unfamiliar readers might think a poet would employ linguistic fireworks to depict so much energy—but not Shumaker. Since her first book, she has developed a cunning combination of conventional form and low-pitched voice. Together these traits help her to register a thorough appreciation of the natural world and an intensive bonding with other human beings. The newest poems, especially those dedicated to Eva Saulitis, the deceased marine biologist turned naturalist poet and memoirist, are—in their precise articulation of free affection—unlike any literary poetry being written today.

As this volume of new and selected poems demonstrates, Shumaker arrived at her current practice by first paying close attention to myriad nuances of organization and sound. In "October, Snow," a highly representative poem from her surprisingly sophisticated first book *Esperanza's Hair*, the language intimates a multilayered relation to landscape. What happens outside of us happens inside of us:

Quiet snow takes on
the shape of the black branch
that's taking on snow.

This low
along the horizon,
the sun

seems hurt,
glazes one birch in last light.
First ice

across the Chena edges out
until two sharpnesses
wound each other into binding.

Dry snow gives way
to the slightest urgings. One black seed
ticks through the crust.

By tracking changes in the snow, the poem renders the way change occurs in the individual. The repeating sounds of "October, Snow" virtually teach us how to read slowly, so as to chronicle the full spectrum of transformation. In the first stanza alone, the words snow and on in the first line are both repeated in the third. Takes returns in the third line as taking. The hard a of the word shape in the second line returns in taking as well. Then there's the light alliteration of black branch; note how the n in branch is a soft echo of the n-sound in the repeated key word snow. Not only do these gently stirring vocalizations suggest care but they also reinforce the importance of our attending to the outside world, a realm that in Shumaker's view tells us so much about ourselves.

Shumaker often prefers short lines comprising short stanzas, which themselves may enact a kind of stillness—as if profound feeling is best measured in an utterance that is closer to felt thought than heard speech. Was it Nat Hentoff who said jazz vibraphonist Milt Jackson knew how to manipulate his notes so that the silence between each was virtually as telling as the note itself? Similarly, from the first of Shumaker's books, there exists a blend of imagery, sound, and arrangement that's at once highly imaginative and quietly discreet. In "October, Snow," for instance, note how the line breaks enhance the relation between the second and third stanzas. While each line complicates the previous line, the meticulous breaks make each line an intriguing unit of expression. Like that silence between the notes of the vibraphone, there's a brief silence enacted at the end of each line (i.e., "low / along" or "light. / First"), not simply slowing the pace but mimicking the way the attentive mind recognizes both the details and the implications of the thing seen.

Ultimately, Shumaker's talent for rendering such exacting perception has come to enrich poems about close friendships. Her deft use of sound and silence paradoxically allows readers to sense the wide, textured, complex inner lives of self and others. Shumaker reminds us that we don't need to shout to assert feeling. She's created a language that is both nuanced and sensual, and these qualities can serve to aerify readers—that is, open their minds to new possibilities in the way we relate to others. The result is often a capacious gratitude for those close to us.

Robert Frost famously said that poetry happens "when an emotion has found its thought and the thought has found words." But even most of Frost's poems are shadowed by an elegiac submission to the indifferent whims of nature. In this manner his emotions are pre-attenuated. Like Frost, Shumaker has a realistic view of nature, but she's not one to slip into a confining voice. True, she's described how nature can harm. But few poets are as persuasive in depicting nature as an astonishingly beautiful template. Her later poems gain an even further resolve about the need for inclusion and affection.

Radical in its open-hearted declarations of human affinity, the recent "Geology of Wonder" is a seven-section sequence, and each section seems like the individual rock of a cairn. The remarkably expansive poem starts by reminding us that we are "shaped gradually by grinding, / shaped over eons by rivers of ice" and that "this mountain changes each breath." The poem is an elegy afloat on grateful memories in which Shumaker remembers two close female friends, Judith Kitchen and Eva Saulitis. Its fourth section links the outer world of nature to the inner world of the individual who has come to look outside of herself:

> When the horizon holds on
> to the sun, when light
> lingers and dim shapes
> gather in every ravine
>
> alpenglow eases
> first out of snowbanks
> then out of cloudscapes
> then out of our eyes

into stars closer now because
we have stepped out from under
whatever we call shelter
to be with the sky.

And in a poem that charts the paths of two women who have already died as well as her own conscious path toward the inevitable end, she finds in the sixth section that the world around us is a refuge for virtue, awe, and mystification:

Radical, our innocence,
as in rooted,
as all that matters
pushes up from that root

toward light, as each moment
spreads wide to gather moisture,
as our wonder tunnels deeper,
riddles rich earth.

Most important, Shumaker connects that appreciation of natural beauty to an appreciation of interconnected human lives lived well. The cairn, a mound of rocks arranged by individuals as a marker or memorial for someone else, is a strikingly apt symbol.

Most readers come to poetry to transcend the quotidian, to experience a voice other than their own, and thus to participate more fully in human experience. The poems in this collection understand that the highest form of such participation requires self-transformation. Shumaker is like Rainer Maria Rilke, who famously ended "Archaic Torso of Apollo" by claiming, "You must change your life." But where Rilke wanted the reader to become more inner-directed, Shumaker's poems usually ask us to turn outward in order to recognize the numinous humanity of people in our lives. A woman writing against a tradition of austere male expression, she makes poetry that insists on the primacy of love and the attendant need to express that love.

Shumaker certainly realizes that the human animal is crosscut by two passions: to bond and to brutalize. As a result, her poems gain a hard-earned tension from the way civilization approaches human and environmental frailty on one hand and the way she believes we can change our behavior on the other. Unlike many poets who succumb to visions of dystopic inevitability, she asserts both hope and personal responsibility. She rejects the tempting cynicism that presently marks sociopolitical discourse in person, online, or in the media, proposing instead a new, more confident polemic. At the steady center of her radical writer's ethos, she understands that the world is more than a locale for crude or inhumane behavior. Taken together, the poems in this volume form a kind of verse cairn, each standing for what the poet proposes as countering traits: a tough-skinned tenderness, a predilection to joy, and an impulse toward celebration.

—Kevin Clark

NEW POEMS

PARENTHOOD, UNPLANNED

When a jasmine-scented
teenager (not yet my mother)

came up pregnant
with me, my father

stepped up.
They did what teenagers did

in 1951. Married.
Mismatched

spectacularly—
fifteen years of yelling and beer.

Four kids and two
miscarriages

before she turned
twenty-four.

No education
past high school.

So after the divorce,
crap jobs,

crappier men,
government cheese,

no sleep.
Haunted, her eyes.

There are men
making decisions

right now
about lives of girls

and women.
Some do not want

children to know
how their bodies work.

Some do not trust
women to make

decisions. As if
women were people,

as if women
know what's best

for their lives,
for the lives

of their children.
That broken teen

who carried me, who
pushed me out

into this world,
that brilliant

ragged girl
died young, worn down

in her thirties.
One small life,

I know. The only life
she had. I speak for her

when I say
Let women live.

Let women be.

Stepped Ice, Barry McWayne

STOP BATH

in honor of Barry McWayne

How many winters did you
traipse through snow to the riverbank,

toting tripod, lenses, filters,
new body? How many times

did you check the light,
wait in hard cold,

check again, stiff fingers
barely curled around the camera?

How many bends and riffles
tripped you, brittle weeds

held fast? How much overflow
crept out from under ice,

hardened, gushed, seeped,
froze? How many years looking

before you framed these
crusted steps of ice

stopped in silver gelatin?
How many times did you point out

on archival paper
what's right here

under our
frost-nipped toes,

look—

PLACING OUR FEET WITH CARE ON THIS EARTH

in honor of Eloise Klein Healy & Colleen Rooney

SHAPE-SHIFTERS

One morning a poet wakes,
reaches for her beloved, speaks

with passion
pure nonsense.

The partner, startled
from sleep,

can't put together
their garbled situation.

Her woman, self-made,
who shaped herself with words

has now reworded
her fluent tongue, chopped

word-parts tongue whipped
till she's giving voice to shards,

shattered sounds not yet
nor ever connected.

Why? The best guesses
still guesses, microscopic.

Who are we without sounds
someone we love can translate

into us,
into what we know

of ourselves?

O inflamed brain.
O heart afire.

Who are we without language?

THE ONE WAITING

For years she's read about the brain,
all the fine science she could find,

probing neurons and synapses,
folds unfolding, refolding,

wanting all that gray to matter
in new ways, wanting

secrets unfolded, refolding
vision, movement, emotion,

memory, aroma, language
within lobes and layers

that travel back
to our reptile selves.

How do we smell
food? How do we feel

love? Ancient
basic brain sparks.

Two hemispheres, one world.
World of how we dance,

what we contain, what we can
and can't recall. What we can

and cannot conjure, say.
Her world, her love

has trespassers
in her brain, microbes

tracking up
the wilderness of her mind,

her fine wild mind.
She must, the doctors tell her,

wait.

Wait.
And see.

Too much insight
her reading offers.

What she can't
admit

crushes her, packs her
skull tight.

Scary, all
she knows.

Scary, all she
cannot know.

Edgy, flayed,
facing borders

she doesn't want
to cross.

So afraid. Tender.
She can't

let herself count
by the thousands

all the intricate
spiraling losses,

all the shades
on the color wheel of terror,

all the galling
flavors of grief.

THE POEMS YOU CANNOT WRITE RIGHT NOW

May they wait
within you.
Wait while your body

sluffs off its trespassers,
while your wild mind
returns from the tangle

you've been wandering.
May they arrive
like migrants

in their own good time,
hungry
from their long flight,

ready to nest,
brood, nurture
the next generation.

RIVER ICE

Warm aroma of windowsill
basil, rosemary, oregano,

two stories above
the frozen river.

Mica glints on tracked snow,
light puddles

where warmth
has turned winter

to water. And you
on your own white expanse

finding your way
no map or path

you creating the path
first by breath

then by glances
glinting between

you and the one
who waits

who has for twenty-eight
winters waited

with you, knowing
the great migrations

swirled, winged motion
turning as the earth tilts

and turns, the Arctic terns
returning far north from

Tierra del Fuego
and you're with them,

returning this season
after trial by fire

tempered by your plunge
into icy waters,

oh woman forged anew
your wings

conducting heat,
harsh music of melting,

solid river cracked and unstable
soon to turn liquid

electrons stirring,
phoenix flexing.

BABY STEPS

Steps. Of any kind.
Impossible.

At least today.
Try again

tomorrow.
You, reclined,

your hurt brain

interrupted.
Turning

in bed
would spell

improvement.
Sitting up

a distant goal.
Concentrating

even one inning
even one out

of a Dodgers game
something you'll

get back.
Feeding on hope,

we picture you
feeding yourself

one day,
swallowing

strength
we wish for you

with each spoonful,
then saying out loud

with your great
raucous laugh, "Thanks!"

or any word
we might understand.

FRAGILE

One person redefined,
moon-cooled young ice

built in calmness to grease ice
built in agitation to shuga,

fine spicules stacked to frazil,
frazil hardened to floes,

floes carved by sea
to hanging shelves,

bergy bits and growler ice
crackling, brash wreckage

crashing through nilas ice,
its crust elastic, shaping

to swells that fall away
as quickly as they rise.

Every year snow
collected on the glacier

another layer
of pollen, another record

of how we treated
one another

and our home,
how our earth

pressured beyond holding
erupted undersea

then into air, and the ash,
some of it, settled

here on the ice
where it wouldn't be discovered

till core sample slices
scoped in the lab

revealed truths too small
for us to see, revealed

lives our size, lives
large as oceans frozen

until sunwarmed
ice candles, crisp jangles,

returned to sea
taking with them

memories of how it felt
to be magma, lava, steam,

snowflake, glacier,
what it meant to feel

one's rind
slush off,

one's chilled mind
begin again,

all over again
to take unpredictable shape.

SPECIAL EFFECTS

Daughter of a father in the business,
father who created the wind,

father who before computers
generated illusions,

father who masterminded
storms, floods, explosions

set to do no harm, not even
to throw much more

than dust
or smoke.

Working-class daughter
working now

to speak. Everyday words
lounge around like extras

costumed, positioned,
waiting,

no lines, the scene
set, clapperboards clacked.

Her lines. The whole script.
Shredded. Ad-lib

our whole lives. Making it up
as we go.

That it should be easy
the great illusion.

THEY HAD MORNINGS IN THOSE DAYS

Dawns when first light washed
over treetops in Ecuador, their binocs

focused, each leaf outlined,
species they traveled far to visit

vocal among branches.
Ay, the turquoise

jay, the collared Inca
hummingbird, whirring,

green feathers
slick with day.

Step by step
their footfalls awoke

aromas in first-growth
rainforest, drops poised,

swelling on drip tips
then plashing

softly as whispers
between lovers,

their lower lips
held between teeth as they

pointed, silently, toward
the sound of sunrise,

cry of the golden-headed
quetzal—there, maybe? There?—

How what eludes us
keeps its hold,

deepens
our desire.

PLACING OUR FEET WITH CARE ON THIS EARTH

In Los Angeles, my friend will soon learn to walk.
Her ankles will remember how to line up

so her weight can settle down
and they can hold up.

In Alaska, snowmelt's ankle-deep
slush puddles firm up overnight.

Slick, this world. Our soles
get away from us.

HOW TO LIVE

Before you speak think
about what the person

struggling to speak
wishes to say.

Before you rush think
about how dawdling

lets you see
along the scum line

at the beach
tangles

easy to ignore,
lets you sort out

abalone shells
snarled in kelp, layer

upon layer, pearl shine
rinsed in brine.

Before you heave
body spent

onto wet sand,
glance up—

backlit pelicans
skim over breakers,

red skeletons
in each wing

outlined by the sun
they block.

Thirst. Remember thirst.
Offer water, always.

Then swallow
ocean air, swallow

clean water. Cherish
what made you.

The hard parts
and the tender.

THE BASICS

How the spoon dips into the bowl.
How it finds its way to the lips.
How lips open, in time.

How the body cries out.
How it must. How it cannot.
How we lift what we cannot lift.

How generous, allowing help.
How we don't want to need.
How we all need.

How touch heals.
How love touch
makes us human.

How we forget what we know.
How we learn again.
How we forget what we wanted.

How what we want evolves.
How that mammoth we were stalking got away.
How this salmon, plump with eggs, returns.

OTHER DAYS

When the therapist asks *Can you*
hand me the red one? some days
she can. Other days,
not so much. Other days

her strings of syllables
haunt the air, shared
words dear, most dearly
departed. Other days,

the morning
paper makes no sense,
the morning
might as well be midnight.

Dawning's a continent
distant and iced,
explorers starved,
perishing.

But one day
without a word
of warning
she wakes,

stretches,
says just like that
Guess I better
get up.

A MEDITATION

Come closer. Ask your foot to widen
as it meets the floor.

Ask twin handrails
to lead you on.

Flirt. Play
with your food.

Be hands-on
with your love.

Touch your tongue
to your teeth, fire pose.

Breathe in
breathe out.

Relax
until language remembers you,

relax
until words bask in your light.

HEALING

What we cannot yet reach
what we cannot yet do

the *yet* means we're alive.

Wild frustration, growing.

What we cannot ever reach
what we cannot ever do

the *ever* means we're human.

ANYONE WHO COMES HERE MUST BE TRANSFORMED

Whether hatched from a shell
brittle or leathery,

whether launched
down that muscular slide,

whether blown in
on winds prevailing,

anyone who arrives here
must be transformed.

Toward dusk, take your ease.
Drop anchor for the night.

Cry out and see what others provide.
To your lips your beloved must lift

morsels warm and
soft as muscles unmoved.

Late in life, after much pain,
this beloved

touched down, stranger
your heart awaited

always, the blank space
in you reshaped

to her dimensions.
And hers to yours.

Now you make room—
room for words

that take sweet time
surfacing, room

for hands that tremble
when they cannot grasp

the simplest cup.
Together

you learn again
how to breathe, eat, drink,

how to walk on surfaces smooth
or rocky, how to cook up

ways to crack the other up.
Together you refine

loss's life-giving
language—

how to keep love
laughing.

COMMONPLACE MIRACLES

1.

Thanks for impatience
married to dogged will,

gratitude for grit,
for the uneaten bits

of her brain leaping
toward whatever they can find

cellular frenzy
orb of herring

churning
bait ball

brain luring
something large.

2.

Praise for her eyes
open, at peace.

Her eyes, rabid
to speak

when words don't work.
Her eyes,

tracking a high fly
over and out

into the great beyond,
that tangle of weeds

behind the ball field.

YES, BEFORE

So much we didn't have to think about
back then, back when

we didn't consider
muscular complexities

of kisses, comments, concepts.
Time and materials,

fixing up the house we share,
making it more our own

before. And now, after,
how now do we shape

these lives allotted us, lives
stranger than any stranger,

strange as all we held
and never knew

before. And now, our own
wilderness becoming us.

Giving back, piece by piece,
what the other trusted us to keep.

ROPE NECK THING

Once this woman could speak
one syllable only,

the rest of her restless
vocabulary wild

inside her, a pack
of Portuguese water dogs

loping, whirling,
dust devil of words

she could not catch
up to, words she could hear

but could not call, words
that evaporated, blurred

dog dreams she wanted to save
to tell her beloved.

On this day, this woman stood,
gave her poems voice, her voice

running back when it was called,
bounding, ecstatic to see her.

Later, walking and talking
(at once!) we speak of her darling

Nikita. "She's so good, sometimes,
sometimes she doesn't need

the rope neck thing." I praise
the mischievous one who gnawed

everything her teeth could grab,
the pup who swallowed rocks,

the one who never minded,
who treated her people as chew toys:

"Nikita stays with you sometimes
without a leash!" Eloise nods, "Yes, no leash."

And I see at her heel all the poems
she's yet to write, tagging along, catching up.

SPARKS

A CONVERSATION IN POEMS AND PAINTINGS

paintings by Kesler E. Woodward

Two friends decided to share a yearlong artistic conversation. Kes Woodward asked Peggy Shumaker to write a poem, and he created a painting in response to it. Peggy wrote in response, Kes painted in response, again and again. As each piece added its vividness to the conversation, both writer and artist found they were responding not just to the last piece but to the entire body of work. The work took many unpredictable and startling turns, adding to the intensity of this third art—an art that's not language alone, not purely painting, but a bonding of the two.

The conversation was made public at an exhibition at the Alaska Humanities Forum, in a special feature of *Alaska Quarterly Review,* and at www.aqreview.org/special-feature-sparks-a-conversation-in-poems-and-paintings.

Kes Woodward received the first Alaska Governor's Award for Lifetime Achievement in the Arts in 2004, and he was named a Rasmuson Foundation Distinguished Artist in 2012. His artwork is represented in all of Alaska's major public art collections and in museum, corporate, and private collections on both coasts of the United States. An emeritus professor of art, he retired in 2000 from the University of Alaska Fairbanks in order to work in his studio full time. Please visit his website at www.keslerwoodward.com.

THE CONVERSATION

KES WOODWARD: We decided at the very beginning that this would be a true conversation. I suggested that she write a poem and I make a painting in response to it, and she make a poem in response to that painting, and I make another painting in response to that one, and we'd just see where it went. What we showed at the Alaska Humanities Forum in September 2015 was the result of that almost yearlong conversation between a poet and a painter.

PEGGY SHUMAKER: Early on we decided independently and then together that anything that came up was fair game and we would include it. Kes said that usually when he does a show there is some continuity in terms of either material or size or subject matter. But this time he chose many different media, many different sizes, and many different subjects. The poems came in different forms and with a wide range of concerns. Each artwork focused our attention in distinct ways, and we let everything in, just as you might in a conversation with a friend.

KES WOODWARD: That was one of the most exciting things about it. Probably the most exciting thing was that we didn't know, going into it, where it would lead, and we certainly could never have predicted what we would come up with when we began.

PEGGY SHUMAKER: It was absolutely thrilling to see it all in one place, because during the show at the Alaska Humanities Forum, that was the first time anybody had seen all the poems and paintings together.

KES WOODWARD: Including us [*laughing*].

PEGGY SHUMAKER: Yeah [*laughing*]. So that was pretty wonderful.

KES WOODWARD: So . . . we started with one of Peggy's poems.

PEGGY SHUMAKER: Yes. This poem came from a memory of a dance performance by a woman named Maureen Fleming. One of her specialties is moving exquisitely slowly.

THREE BLUES

after Maureen Fleming

We once watched a woman
naked with grace fall
down a flight

of stairs so steep
no Dall sheep
could balance there,

set of stairs built precisely
for falling. The woman
had trained body

and soul to fall

exquisitely

slowly

sculpting

light

each movement melting
into the next
so that time

held its breath.
The eye could not trust
what it couldn't see

gestures so quiet
they register only after
we notice their passing.

Her falling took infinity
along for the ride, her spine
knobby testament

to all we must imagine,
dancing shape of galaxies
sending tendrils of stardust

to breathe in dark matter
where we live incompletely
aware one moment.

Paints wet on the palette,
brush tip blending
three blues with a touch

of black, slow swirl graceful
and sure, painting past knowing,
painting into all we cannot touch.

KES WOODWARD: For this poem and all the others, I received the poem from Peggy, and I read it, and I took a deep breath, and I went on working on whatever I was working on. I posted it on the wall in my studio, and every day when I came into the studio, I would read the poem. Then I would try to put it out of my mind and work on whatever I was going to work on and wait for a response to come. And sure enough and very, very rapidly in this case, I knew in general terms how I wanted to respond to it.

What I came up with was a painting called *Three Blues* from one of the last lines in the poem. That's the most obvious way that it relates to the poem—the three blues blended with the brush tip with a touch of black is very much a part of the image that you see. But the poem itself seemed to be mostly about precipitousness, steepness, the possibility of falling. And the most precipitous place I've ever been, the steepest place I've ever been, and the most dramatic place I've ever been is a place called the Sheldon Hut, which is atop a two-hundred-foot rock outcropping in the middle of Ruth Glacier, six miles as the crow flies from the summit of Denali. Dorli and I spent five nights there three years ago in May and were just bowled over by the place. That image came immediately to mind after reading Peggy's poem. And so I focused on that quality of steepness, on the blending of the blues, on the blacks, but not illustrating. None of the images that I made for the show are illustrations of Peggy's poems, and none of Peggy's poems are illustrations of my paintings. They are simply responses to them that in my case, at least, came unbidden in response to my reaction to the poems, given the time for them to sink into my consciousness and elicit some kind of response.

Three Blues: Mt. Dickey from the Sheldon Hut (oil on paper, 28″ x 40″)

PEGGY SHUMAKER: Once I looked at Kes's painting (by the way, at this stage we were in different cities and so I didn't see his work in person; I saw it as an image on the computer screen), I found it extremely dramatic. It's filled with severe opportunities to fall. It's filled with geologic outcroppings. It's filled with a sense of something much larger than ourselves.

And so for the next piece, I wrote a little poem and then another little poem and another little poem, and the piece just kept building in the way that some mountains build. Not all, but some. My sense of what we can't quite grasp is very large in this poem.

My friends have begun to die. That's a hard sentence, a hard circumstance. Sometimes we become more fully ourselves as we face this, feel this, think about this.

In this poem, several people make cameo appearances: Sherry Simpson (the young writer), my beloved Joe, Judith Kitchen and Stan Rubin, and Eva Saulitis.

GEOLOGY OF WONDER

1.

Shaped by forces way underneath,
shaped gradually by grinding,
shaped over eons by rivers of ice,
shaped by wind, by rain, by eruption, by season
after season of snow, some melting, some packing down
evidence of how this mountain came to be
what it is this instant, how
this mountain changes each breath

2.

A young writer once asked
a roomful of writers to list

our fears. To start us,
she jotted on the board

bears
blindness
widowhood

Until that moment I had not
let myself know

that I too carry inside a little nugget
of preemptive mourning

for our hardy and loving bond, for the days
of our marriage forged late in life

a marriage that cannot last

because we cannot last

3.

Over years of working for each breath,
Judith made files,
files to help Stan

find his way
once she wasn't there
to holler and guide him.

One file lists women
he should and should not
date. With reasons,

juicy
and funny.
I can just see her

amusing herself
amassing this catalog
of poignance,

antidote
to the loneliness
of dying.

4.

When the horizon holds on
to the sun, when light
lingers and dim shapes
gather in every ravine

alpenglow eases
first out of snowbanks
then out of cloudscapes
then out of our eyes

into stars closer now because
we have stepped out from under
whatever we call shelter
to be with the sky.

5.

Aware that death
draws very close, dear Eva
lives parallel lives.

One involves *next*—
next whale season, next
harvest of honey and kale,
next visit with grandson Findlay,
next birthday.

One involves *last*,
as desires sharpen
then fall away.
Last hike up Grace Ridge,
last trip to Latvia, last
manuscript complete.

Each word
next to last
she writes.

6.

Radical, our innocence,
as in rooted,
as all that matters
pushes up from that root

toward light, as each moment
spreads wide to gather moisture,
as our wonder tunnels deeper,
riddles rich earth.

7.

We must stand far off
or go up in a plane
to see much of this mountain.

When we're on it,
our focus shifts
to scree underfoot,

to a shady cornice
overhanging our steps,
to a patch of lichen

breaking
down
stone.

The view
vast
beyond us.

KES WOODWARD: So that poem, longer than the rest in this conversation, elicited not one but two paintings—a larger one I called *Horizon Holds On* and a smaller one called *Vespertine*. Both of them come from essentially the same place. They're very similar images, from the neighborhood where Dorli and I live. We walk our dog along a ridge that overlooks the city. In the far distance, you can see on a good day, not only the alpenglow and the mountains of the Alaska Range and the Tanana Valley basin, but Denali off in the distance on the horizon, just over the top of Chena Ridge.

One of the things that neither of us anticipated, I think, was how much of this conversation would be influenced by the fact that we're growing older, and we're feeling our age. We have friends who are undergoing great trials. We have friends like Eva, who is nearing the end of a long trial. And we have become very, very aware of the temporariness of life . . . the tentativeness of life and the impossibility of holding on. In February in Fairbanks the tentativeness of the light, the way the sun comes up just barely east of due south, crawls above the horizon almost on it, and then drops out of sight, became a really strong metaphor for me of that sort of tenuousness of life and the way the light tries to hold on to the horizon. And so this painting, both these paintings, came very much out of a response to that growing theme that was emerging in the conversation as a whole and the references in this specific poem.

Horizon Holds On: Denali from Taiga (acrylic on canvas, 30″ x 40″)

Vespertine (acrylic on canvas, 20″ x 16″)

PEGGY SHUMAKER: I was thinking, too, as I looked at these paintings, both of them, how in this atmosphere of tenuousness, it becomes vitally important for us to make human connections. Questions of distance and perspective, and how distance alters perspective, stretched out before me. I have a nephew who at the age of seventeen met his father for the first time. And I was thinking about how dramatic that distance has been for them and then what it meant for them actually to be in the same room and to be able to touch one another. This one's called "Sun at the Horizon."

SUN AT THE HORIZON

for Malik and Dorrell

His whole life, the boy suffered
having no dad. His sister had one
in the house for a while
but he hit. Never
his, never real, never dad.

In the story his mom tells
he was conceived
far north in the month
light returns, sifted
by branches of black
spruce and birches
long since bare.

Far, the mountain
so high it changes weather.
Far, the distance—
who he is, who
he might be. When he stands
taller than his mother,
slim and strong as a fresh
trunk of birch,
he flies east to meet

the man he has imagined,
the man defined by absence,
the man who was half his making,
the man he hated when he needed
him most, the man he has wanted
more than anyone to love,
the man who holds what he needs
to know, the man whose silence
echoes his silence.

When the plane touches down
his stomach lurches. He walks
the unfamiliar path
to baggage claim. Through
the milling crowd, one man—
around him, his father's arms—
light after long darkness

returning to the world
all the branches the dark time
has hidden, iced rivers braided,
the legacy of sky opening, the self
a shape-shifting cloud, backlit.

KES WOODWARD: So what was wonderful about getting to see all these paintings and poems together for the first time was being able to look back and forth and see the way that the poem makes references to the image before it, and then to think about what I was thinking about as I made the painting in response to it. And in many ways, it's all there. It's all there in both of them. That poem is very much about individuals and relationships among people and relationships in families.

Birches, in my work, have always stood in for people, in their individuality and their uprightness, their strength and their fragileness, and their vulnerability. Things that happen to them in their lives show as scars in their bark, the same as scars on our skin. And groups of birches have often in my work been in my mind family portraits. Larger ones, smaller ones, younger ones, older ones. Images of relationships and individuals and aging. And so, naturally enough, I turned in response to that poem to a multiple image of birch trunks and branches and to the numerous references to branches. There's a reference to a branch, to an arm being put around. There are young people, and there are older people, and there are relationships among them. And there is a bareness to the branches that is referenced a number of times in the poem. That is very much the case with most of the birches that I paint and particularly in the birches that I chose for this painting. But there is also in the poem this sense of reawakening hope as this contact is made. I was making this painting in the spring, when the leaf buds on the trees were just warming and swelling and just about to burst, and so I was eager to include those leaf buds in the painting, just about to swell and burst into life in response to the gathering of this family.

Birches Bare (acrylic on canvas, 48″ x 60″)

PEGGY SHUMAKER: It was absolutely marvelous that I got to go to Kes's studio and see this painting. I also got to see the paintings that came before, and I think that enlarged the conversation for me in a great many ways. Kes's paintings, when you see them on a computer screen, are gorgeous, but you're seeing one portion, one facet of the painting. When you see them in person, when you get up close, you savor a highly textured, abstract experience. When you stand six feet away, you see different elements and notice different relationships. And when you stand across the room the paintings resolve into images in ways that they don't when you're right up next to them, as close as Kes would be while painting. I got to see lots of lines and shapes that looked like maps in this painting when I was up close.

In the far north, we have a term for the day the leaves break open—green up. After six or seven months of snow and ice, spring rushes in, extravagant in its promise. Ice breaks up on the river. Nasal passages thaw out and aromas return. So do songbirds, swans, ducks, geese. Layer by layer, we emerge after hard cold.

The poem also involves a concert by a flute choir. Dorli, Kes's wife, has for over thirty-five years led a flute choir. This year, for one of the pieces, she taught her flutists to aim air through their flutes so that it makes a really haunting and powerful vibration but no tone. It's not a note. It's just quickened air gliding through tubes. It's incredibly beautiful. So that's in here as well.

And then I found out one other thing. When I was looking at the surfaces of old paintings, thinking about them, I realized there has to be a word for what happens when the paint can't hold together anymore. And there is! That juicy word made it into the poem. Kes probably knew that word all along [*laughing*].

GREEN UP

Iris shoots shin tall
pierced ground
a week ago.

All the buds holding tight,
birch, chokecherry, alder,
have broken,

green filling in
all the blanks on the map.
Spring's privacy

shields songbirds
trilling for territory,
jazzing for mates.

Scrolls of bark reveal
the cartographer's art—
how the city of each tree

sprawls, layered,
intricate apartments
occupied by pollen

drifting on breath,
burgeoning air of a flute choir
angled so the tremble

translates tension
traveling
lung to hollow

to the open ear
of the world, the curve
of the alto doubling

the thrill,
air channeled to art,
no tone, no note

restraint just burst.
Two steps back
birch branches blacken.

Two steps forward
birch branches
crackle, the dark palette

of a beloved addict
about to be released,
unsure, consumed

with all the shades
of what's next, knowing only
how this season

sends tiny fissures
across every
surface, the craquelure

of self.
Spring leads us on,
lets us divine

elaborate patterns
of cracks
we call ourselves,

all the broken
places that make us
us.

KES WOODWARD: At this point in this developing conversation, things started to get weirder and eerier in a wonderful way. My paintings began to respond to the poems in ways that I didn't anticipate, and even more than usual, my paintings felt out of my control. This painting is one of the most striking examples of that that I can remember in my work. It's called *Spring Leads Us On*, and it's not at all the painting that I set out to make. I started to make a painting about green up, because that's the poem that preceded it. And it was very much a poem about burgeoning life and spring and greening up, and I thought, "Great! So I'm going to look up. I'm going to look up into the trees, and I'm going to celebrate the leaves coming out on the trees and focus on the underside of the canopy." And I started working on the painting, and it got away from me. Instead of being spring, it turned into summer, and then before I knew it, it turned into fall. And as I kept on, every day I would come back into the studio and as I was working on the painting, I would read the poem again. But I kept thinking, you know, what's happening here? Why is this painting not about green up? Why is this painting not about spring? Why is it turning into fall? It wasn't until I was nearly done with the painting, and it was very much a fall painting, that I realized that it was spring leading us on. I thought about how when it's spring, you think the summer's going to last forever. And when you're young, you think life is going to last forever.

At the time I was working on this painting, my son's partner turned thirty, and my son was just about to turn thirty a couple of months later. I talked to Becca, his partner, and I said, "You know, I remember turning thirty. I remember being in my office at the university and my good friend Glen Simpson, who is exactly ten years older than I am, was turning forty just a couple of days later, and I was talking about turning thirty. And that was only yesterday. I swear it was only yesterday." And I told her that [*laughing*]. I'm not sure she wanted to hear that as she turned thirty [*laughing*], that in a day she'd be my age, but it suddenly occurred—so I went back and I read the poem and I saw that line, "Spring leads us on," and I thought, "You know, that's exactly what this is about. This is about how you don't realize as life goes along that it goes by so quickly. And you look back to when you were young and it was just yesterday."

Spring Leads Us On (oil on canvas, 16″ x 20″)

PEGGY SHUMAKER: As Kes mentioned, both of us are of a certain age. My beloved is in his late seventies and I am in my sixties. And I thought that I would be writing a poem—in fact I started drafts of poems—that dealt with particular loved ones who are not around anymore. Not breathing. And then I thought, no, this needs to be a poem of wider human experience, a poem of public engagement. So maybe this one shouldn't be linked to any one individual, even though I had several cherished loved ones in my mind and heart. And I was thinking as I was writing of a Mayan belief that the dead, the living, and those yet to live travel along the roots, trunk, and branches of one enormous tree. I leapt from that image into new possibilities. I began to think about how love continues even when a person's life does not.

LISTENING AMONG BIRCHES

Those of us still rooted to this earth
lie back on the sponge of other lives,
look up through thirteen layers of breath.

Below, roots echo
branching canopies,
deepen and widen

toward moisture
not light. Under us,
nine worlds. At least.

Those who've gone before
travel along trees,
all trees, not

just the giant
the Mayans imagined,
not just the ancient

redwood or kauri
or oak. These birches
hold the laughter

we can't quite call back,
the glance
that touched us

more intimately than skin.
Inside us conversations
continue, layer

upon layer, off-kilter
but not really one-sided, absent
love so fully present.

So much left
unsaid, undone.
Each weight specific.

One love, particular.
Listening alive
beyond mere death.

KES WOODWARD: So in *Springfall: Listening*, this aspen leaf lies back and looks up into the branches, just the way Peggy talks about in the poem. And it lies on the sponge of other lives. It lies on the detritus of the forest. A lot of what was happening in this conversation was our thinking about losses and potential future losses of loved ones. At this point it was still early summer, and this was an aspen leaf that was still green and had fallen before its time. Rain had fallen on it, and raindrops were beaded up on the surface of the leaf. Dorli and I run on paths out our back door and through the boreal forest for six miles on trails every other day, all year round. And I had seen this leaf, or one very much like it, on the path with little beaded-up droplets of rain just a few days before and had thought about how I might want to make a painting of it in some way. And this poem came along, and there was a kind of shock of recognition when I read it. It seemed so much of what that was about. It was about someone fallen, something fallen before its time. It was about something falling in the spring and that concatenation of seasons.

The problem with paintings is that they take a long time to do. I was working on paintings all along, and I would do a painting and I would spend weeks, sometimes six weeks, working on a painting, and then I'd be very pleased to send it off, send an image of it to Peggy, wherever she was, and then two days later a poem would come back [*laughing*], and I would think, "Oh, no, this is too fast! I'm not ready." But then sure enough, you know, I would be off, veering in another direction in response to it.

When I do these paintings, I lay in the image very loosely, and then I go back in and I sort of excavate the detail out of them. I go back in with a tiny brush, and I bring structure and organization. Particularly in something like *Springfall: Listening*, an image that's so intricate. Dorli saw this one when it had just been started, and it was all very diffuse and she said, "Oh, my gosh. You've really sentenced yourself to a long excavation here." And sure enough, I was running out of time, and so I pulled a lot of long days and nights working on this fairly large, three-foot-by-four-foot painting of this leaf in order to get it done. I wanted to get it back to Peggy, so we could get one or two more paintings done for the show.

Springfall: Listening (acrylic on canvas, 36″ x 48″)

PEGGY SHUMAKER: And modestly, Kes is not mentioning that he also had a show at Well Street Art Company that involved many of these paintings and others. I went and sat in front of this painting in July for several hours and just drank it in. Kes said that at the opening people kept coming up to him saying, "It must have been so difficult to paint those raindrops." And you'll hear his response in the poem.

This exchange was particularly moving to me because the painting appeared at just about the anniversary of the deaths of Kes's wife Missy and Dorli's husband Barry McWayne. And so those sorrows are intertwined in this poem even though Missy and Barry are not mentioned by name. They are certainly present.

LETTER TO ONE WHO'S GONE BEFORE

Spring span of aspen
fallen too soon,

twig-jam floating
on rusty blue duff.

One leaf on the path
and you're with me.

Knocking down smoke,
pelting drops

calm wildfires
to smolder.

Drizzle's delicious
grace lets us breathe.

From the serrated
edge to narrow roads

all through me, you live
in each cell. Inhale

the intricate civilization
alive in the fragrance of sage.

Nothing is harder to paint
than anything else,

the artist says. *Just look.*
Paint what you see.

What you cannot see
will surface just fine.

Each raindrop bending
the world in its own

curve. And when we step close,
through each raindrop

our lives shape-shift—
the lives we live

flawed and tender, the lives
we dream minus the suffering,

the life where this aching
absence has walked a few steps

down the path.
You are with me.

KES WOODWARD: So as Peggy said, this was right around the time of the fifth anniversary of my dear, beloved wife Missy's sudden death, in the fortieth year of our marriage, and that was very much on my mind. The loss of my friend Barry, Dorli's husband, ten days later was very much on my mind. The fragility of life was an emerging theme in all of this conversation. What I focused on as I began this painting one day was the notion of a path—that you go down the path and you don't know where the path is going to lead, and all you can do is go down the path. So I decided I would do a painting of the path through the boreal forest, and I would try to lighten things up a little bit [*laughing*] because I was having dark thoughts, and we were talking about fragile and dark things. And so I thought, well, I'm going to look up, or I'm going to look down the path toward the future and try to make a hopeful image of a path. And so I began with these birch trees on either side and the path in between them.

I had just laid in the very beginnings of the painting when Peggy called one day in tears and said that she had just been diagnosed with cancer. I just couldn't believe it. I washed out my brushes, and in a total sense of not knowing anything to do, just drove, racing, across town, and I gave her and Joe big hugs. I was overwhelmed by the sense of helplessness that not only were we remembering losses and not only were we worrying about those that we might lose, but we had darkness staring us right in the face.

I went back home, and I went back to work on this painting, and this dark black spruce tree grew up in the path. It had been a summer painting. It turned into a winter painting. And the spruce tree just kind of appeared. I mean, I didn't consciously think "I'm going to make a spruce tree in the path." The spruce tree just grew up out of its own volition. Outside my own volition in the path that I was putting in this painting, there it was.

I looked up, trying to lift my gaze upward, trying to get beyond that tree. But I couldn't see beyond it. It was so big; it was taking up the path. And it was, you know, again, without consciously setting out to do it at all, it was the absolute embodiment of everything I was feeling at the time. And so, this painting resulted. It's called *Darkness in the Path.*

Darkness in the Path (acrylic on canvas, 36″ x 24″)

PEGGY SHUMAKER: When Kes saw one of my poems, I don't remember which one, Kes . . . I think it was when you saw "Listening among Birches," you emailed me and said, "Wow, wow, wow! Oh, wow! I know exactly what I'm going to do." And that is really uncharacteristic of you.

KES WOODWARD: Right.

PEGGY SHUMAKER: And it's uncharacteristic of me when I start a poem to know exactly where it's headed. So when I was looking at this painting and being distraught and bewildered and overwhelmed, I didn't know what was going to happen. I just had this great surge of writing, and I completely took advantage of our conversation and sent Kes a flurry of poems. That wasn't the deal, but he received them graciously and considered them and did his best. This huge surge came from extremity, but I didn't know where it was going to go. I was living so much in the unknown.

SUCCESSION

after diagnosis

Where once there were birches, a path.
Where we wanted a path, this spruce.
The spruce is not ashamed
of its smell, not sorry
for its shape.
This spruce holds on,
a poor self-pruner,
keeping dead branches for decades.

My friend who nearly died this week
holds that health involves
illness and aging.
True health lets us see
who we are. Not busy,
not going doing making.
Just being. If we're lucky
loved and loving.

Zen aroma of rain
washing birch and spruce.

Spiral of needles
dark blue dusted white.

Breathe.

No matter what grows in us.

Breathe.

How else can we live?

Picea mariana—black spruce

PEGGY SHUMAKER: It was peculiar to me when I looked up the Latin name of black spruce that it involves *mariana,* which is . . .

KES WOODWARD: Mariana was Missy's real name [*laughing*].

PEGGY SHUMAKER: So that was chilling. When I got my diagnosis, they told me I have a rare form of cancer called mucinous colloid carcinoma. That involves a shell of mucus around the cancer cells. So of course I thought of scuba diving and parrotfish. A logical leap [*laughing*].

SIDEWAYS WALKING

day before surgery (mucinous colloid carcinoma)

Scientists don't know why exactly
parrotfish at night secrete
a lovely mucous bubble
and rest within it,
secure from bloodsuckers.

Nor do mere mortals know
why some cells hold on past their time, refusing
so much to die that they
put the whole being in danger.
Disease named for claws

sideways walking, my cells take their time
getting weird, spin their cocoons
and kick back. O shape-shifting
breast. I breathe my finite air, hover fascinated
deep in surging salt.

PEGGY SHUMAKER: That was the day before surgery . . .

Okay. I don't know how memories come back to us and I don't know why they come back to us. This next moment happened many decades ago. An event occurred many decades ago, and then here it showed up, and it was extremely vivid. And so it became this next poem.

Kes and I had been talking about how there are certain things that you can do in the much beloved company of others and certain things that you do alone. That's part of this too.

KISS

One evening I kissed
outside a bookstore
a gentle man
I did not know
kissed this man
twisted in a car
parked I did not
love him, kissed
long and deep
a man I did not love
with everything I had
because I missed
a man I once loved
because I missed
the man I would
one day love so hard
my longing
spread across the sky
backlit red
wide and deep.

My own loneliness
I kissed.

I kissed my mother's
loneliness, my father's,
the loneliness
of all our ancestors,
the loneliness of moss,
of cacti, the spiky loneliness
of lizards, of rattlers,
the loneliness
of birch bark, of black
spruce, the solitary
sweeper teetering

over the eddy,
the swirling
loneliness of green
aurora, the loneliness
of starshine on new snow,
the loneliness
dark gray leaning to black
of stormclouds full
of lightning

that loneliness
I kissed.

KES WOODWARD: So by this time it was fall. It was early fall. Every fall, I think how extraordinary it is that the leaves become most beautiful just as they die. Just before they turn brown and crumble and die altogether is when they take on the brilliant color, and they become more beautiful than ever. And so this year, particularly, as Dorli and I walked in the woods, I noticed that the fireweed leaves were particularly brilliant red. I had been gathering them on our walks and on our runs and bringing them back to my studio and pressing them to hold onto, thinking I might do some kind of painting with fireweed leaves. And then I read these three poems. There was Peggy's struggle with her own cancer going on, there was our dear friend Eva Saulitis moving closer and closer to the end of her path. And there were all those other things that had boiled up in our recollections and in our fears and in our memories in the course of this yearlong conversation. And so I decided I would make a painting of these leaves, kind of falling through the air, and I called it *Firefall (for Eva)*.

I thought a lot about how I wanted these leaves to be. Taking the title "Kiss" from the poem, I thought, "Well, maybe they should be touching. Maybe they should be kissing one another." But the poem is not really just about kissing, it's also about loneliness and about being alone and how no matter how many friends you have and no matter how close they are to you and how much they are there for you, there are paths that you end up having to go alone. Death is one of those. And so I thought, "No, I'm going to pack these leaves in as closely as possible, but I'm not going to let them touch each other. I'm going to acknowledge that as they move toward their end, they go alone. And the kiss, if anything, will be the kiss of frost . . . the kiss of frost that's brought the color to their lives even as their lives are nearing their end." And so I just kept painting fireweed leaves and painting fireweed leaves, and packing them in as closely as I could, trying to celebrate the individuality of each leaf and the beauty of each leaf and the beauty not just of the redness but the torn-ness, of the blackened-ness and the tattered-ness of them that is as much a part of their beauty, it seemed to me, as the brilliance of the color.

And finally I reached a point where I thought, "You know, I could squeeze in another leaf or two but it would look awkward." I liked that there was more space in some places than others, and it seemed like the right number of leaves, and so I counted them to see how many leaves I had. It took me about four tries to count them because I kept getting lost, but when I finally counted them I was a little creeped out to realize that there were sixty-four leaves, which is exactly how old I am [*laughing*]. And I didn't think of that as premonitory, but I kind of liked that, that maybe this celebration of the beauty of life as you get older, and the beauty of getting older, was so personal, and that it dealt with so many of the things that Peggy had brought up in her images. The full title of this painting is *Firefall* (*for Eva*). For some time now, Eva has been recognizing and writing about the fact that she knows that the end is near. That was very much on my mind, and very much on Peggy's mind. She was in contact with Eva, and I would see Eva at advisory meetings for the Bunnell Street Art Center in Homer. So this is really a painting for Eva, celebrating her beauty at the very end of her life and hoping we can be anywhere near as beautiful as we make that lonely journey ourselves.

Firefall (*for Eva*) (acrylic on canvas, 36″ x 36″)

PEGGY SHUMAKER: The grace and the exuberance in this painting are very evocative of Eva.

Many of the paintings in this conversation, Kes, are recognizable as your work, but they are distinct as well. They are not the ones that most people would look at and say, "Oh, that's got to be a Kes Woodward."

They are a little different. Same thing with these poems. They're surely mine, and they certainly come from my artistic sensibility. But this conversation took me in directions that I would never have predicted, and that allowed me to be open to things that usually I don't go toward or explore so much.

KES WOODWARD: It definitely did that for both of us. This conversation took both of us places that we hadn't really intended to go and maybe wouldn't have felt comfortable going to if we hadn't been swept up in the midst of it. I had very much the same sense of unpredictability with your poems.

I was talking to our friend Frank Soos about working with Peggy on this project, and I was saying, "You know, I know Peggy's poems so well and these are definitely Peggy's poems, but they are very different in character. And my paintings, I think, are very different in character. They really are taking twists and turns that we never could have anticipated, and that's the great thing about a collaboration of this sort." This has been just an extraordinary one in that respect.

LILT, PATTER, BOUND

Besides the cancer, I am in good health. —Eva Saulitis

You're listening with great care
to your heart, your musician's heart
that needs you to listen,
heart that insists
on being heard

over the rumbles of that splendid
upstart, your magpie brain, always turning over
something most of us overlook,
finding some pure thing
worthy of wonder.

Out in the Sound, watching
for whales, taking in
salt aromas rocking
your laughter cleanses
your tears cleanse.
You bring home
the Sound in each breath.

If there are miracles, you
are one.

You who with your own hands
scooped out last cups of soil
so the handmade-paper box
holding last bits of your mother
might nest gently in earth,

mother who struggled mightily
in her beauty, mother who taught you
to speak her language, but
who could not teach you
to trust a man, mother whose

heartbeat was your first music,
whose voice was your lifelong music,
mother whose life was your song.

Strings of prayer flags fly now
for her, for you.

Candles lit
in her honor. In yours.

Distant notes of an oboe
just beyond our hearing
beckon. We lean toward
sounds we can't take in,
not yet, feel our mouths
opening around ritual
languages no one
can teach us.

Listen. Let us accept
our heart's lilt, heart's patter,
heart's bounding.

Deep breath and a slow letting go,
the aaaaaaaaaaaaaaah that takes with it
what you don't need to carry.

Whatever we're sure of
disappears. Whatever we doubt
disappears.

We walk
into the forest
humming,
our shadows mixing

with shadows
of everyone we love,

those already mica and root,
those still making songs
from salt air among birch.

KES WOODWARD: That poem is such a wonderful summary of so many of the threads of this conversation. I love that poem, and I love the way it draws so many of those threads together. We can weave them into a kind of Veronica's Veil, a kind of cloth.

As I have worked in my studio since the end of this, people keep asking us, you know, is this the end? It's not the end of our collaboration—we've collaborated before, and we'll collaborate again. I don't doubt that in the least. But I think projects have a beginning and an end. This one had a beginning, and I liked that the exhibit gave it a shape and that we had a certain amount of space to work with and a certain amount of time to work. Then it took on a shape of its own.

I miss having those poems to post on my wall to write in response to. I'm going to my studio, as I do every day, and I'm working and I'm painting, but I miss the conversation that we shared all during the course of the year.

PEGGY SHUMAKER: Me, too. I miss our conversation a lot. Thank you, Kes, so much!

IMPOSSIBLE GRACE

in honor of Eva Saulitis

TOUCHING WHAT'S WILD

after a walk with Craig

The woman who spent the afternoon
vaccinating monk seals at the pinniped clinic
offers us lilikoi, just picked, then

we head downhill to Kaloko-Honokōhau
where five sea turtles have
hauled out on a narrow strip of sand,

one just moments ago, still dark,
still slick with seawater,
its pebbled flipper casually tossed

over the carapace of another already warmed,
this turtle nearly dusty, its eyes
closed, every muscle at ease,

easy as we wade shin-deep
sloshing to offer the respect of distance,
knowing that touching some things in this world—

the heiau, the turtles, dolphins, mantas—
is *kapu,*
while touching other things—

seawater, sunbeam, one another—is food,
the nourishment of touch a kind of language,
the language of kindness, the solace

of wildness, of night herons
leaving the kiawe trees
to soar over the fishponds, over

the shallow bay, over
the breakwater, herons unconcerned
that below them, submerged

at the pinnacles, sea turtles hover,
let tangs and cleaner wrasse relieve them
of what to the fish is food but

to the turtles is annoyance, turtles
that draw in creatures that find *them*
delicious, tiger sharks curious

about divers with their bug-eyed
spotlights, their carefully housed cameras
turned now toward the rows of teeth, toward

the triangles of dorsal and tail fins,
one woman cowering, her back
to the shark, so the ancient creature acts

like a baby, curious, mouthing her tank,
taste the best test of the unknown,
but rude slap on the side

and the shark turns, startled,
still not upset, not hunting,
just finding its way in the world, turning

and turning, taking in
what it knows, tasting
what it doesn't yet recognize.

READING OUT LOUD THE WHOLE BOOK

Beneath towering mango trees
we stopped, Eva and I, stopped
our walk and held
each other, sobs
surging through us
like surf, breaking. Breaking
new trail, one step, another,
toward and into
what we could not yet know.
Know this. This one hour
we walked. Walked and
held one another. Another sip
of good company, of calm.
Calm now, our voices
as we turn new leaves,
Eva's still-forming lines
alive. Alive, my voice giving voice
to Eva's words, reading to her
her own prayer-poems.
Prayer-poems we breathed
into the breeze. Breezes carried them
over the island, across the ocean
named for peace. Peace, yes, and rough water.
Water in all her stories. Stories of water,
broken. Broken women, two women
who gave birth only
to words. Words in every cell
of us, healthy or rogue,
words around, above, beneath.

LISTS

Not simple, her lists,
lists she compiled
right to the end, lists
of what she wanted to witness
getting done, lists that she knew
would outlive her.

Her lists at fifteen, running,
taking deep
controlled
oboe breaths, echoed
her lists
thirty years later.

Later on, when she lay
fully aware that later
would not include her
she gave over her lists
to love. Loved ones completed
what they understood,

checked off
each possession that
left the house in the hands
of its new owner,
the chosen one. One ritual
making the list, another

fulfilling each desire.
Desires lined up
in a vertical row, waiting.
Waiting, unlike messy
desires not yet
named, not yet

admitted to, not
admirable or likely, desires
we carry deep. Deep down, where
what we cannot know
about this life, about
our many lives, thrives.

HOLY, THE SOUP

Holy, the soup
each neighbor brings by.
By now, suffering has eased

into our lives, moved in,
taken over. Overnight
we stop expecting next year,

next week, tomorrow.
Tomorrow might as well
be orbiting Saturn,

it's that far
out of reach. Reach
for her gently.

Gently sing a little
off-key the melody
she sang only

when she trusted
you. You know that
dog hair mixed

with her hair
will make you weep
so you leave it, a comfort.

Comfort yourself with small
morsels. Morsels of grief
that begin under the tongue,

then swell, salty,
crash, recede.
Recede into parts of yourself

that you'd nearly forgotten.
Forgotten, the aroma of
lilikoi, the lilt of her

laughter, the longing
for all that's lost. Lost,
and holy.

NO RECIPE

No recipe for this, no chart,
no map, no sense
of how far

we have to go, when we'll know
we've arrived, how we'll recognize
this is the place,

these are our people,
we have a bond, a reason
to care, a responsibility to

make sure we do all
we can to clear the path
for those who pass this way

next, to leave no obstruction, just
the sense that they're not alone, not
the first to make a home

here, not the first
to visit, but the opposite,
to be the one aware of all

who have come before,
shoved out by war, disaster,
disease, spurred on

by adventure
or escape, curiosity
on the cellular level,

each organism doing
what it must
to survive, to thrive, to carry on

what it's been given, to pass along
the best, the worst,
and everything in between,

to make its way
from one span
of mysteries

to another,
that great spiral
opening with each turn.

JANUARY

Ice along Homer Beach.
Snow weighing down alders and birch.

January. Camp robbers,
redpolls, ravens.

Tucked among branches
tucked with love

into the thicket,
woven testament

to human need—
need to mark

and make meaning, need
to make tangible

one particular departure
we can't comprehend

even though
cedar waxwings

gather, welcome
what she had

to leave behind,
tiny bundle of bones,

skin rinsed with rosewater,
the calls of cedar waxwings.

ONE WEEK AFTER

Craig arrives
with a fifty-pound box
of wild-caught salmon
he hauled out of the Kenai, vacuum
sealed, froze, and tucked into Styrofoam
for the long journey
Homer–Anchorage
Anchorage–Kona,
this small coffin
the least of what he carries.

Carries the weariness
of years celebrating
each particle
of hope, each teaspoon
of good news. News
mostly involving
some "new normal,"
the kind of daily
living that means abandoning
ways you used to figure
a day might go, ways
you assumed a life
might go.

Go ahead, go deep.
Deep as killer whales
sounding, deep as the secrets
they keep.
Keep close
the moment that Eva
by some monumental
effort opened
her eyes, held his eyes
with hers and,

already on her way
beyond this life, smiled.
Smiled and drew
breath. Breath that
as it left her body
took Eva along.
Along into inky
cold darkness she craved,
where death,
as she told us,
waited,
perfect and safe.

CHOICES

You chose. For your body's last journey you chose
to have loved ones wash with rosewater
your tiny shape, dress
your delicate bones
in Carhartts and a thick
Latvian sweater, your warmest
wool socks over icy feet, then
you chose to smile toward those
who loved you, those who wove
from willow, alder, birch boughs
what you dubbed "the basket casket,"
casket whose weaving
you witnessed, choosing
these rituals, making them up
as we each make up our lives
as we go along,
yoga chants and snow, tasting
what little the devastated body
could still choose
to take in, you chose to let
Celia, gone ahead years ago, tuck you
into the basket of her dogsled, the snow
brilliant, both of you squinting,
Celia strong and sure
on the runners, her thick gray
braid flying, the trail solid, stretching far, far,
the dogs overjoyed, yipping and panting,
booties keeping ice out
of their pads, dogs pulling hard
in their harnesses, steady pull
uphill and over, all of us waving
till you round the bend,
out of sight, waving.

VALENTINE FOR EVA

Impossible grace,
all the rituals
you created, rituals

that shaped your living,
practices for each letting go—
each person you loved, even

your best beloved,
beehives and garden you could
no longer tend,

the pen
you couldn't hold
to jot notes, lines, images

of whales
battering Dall porpoises
then gorging

though you're not
there to see, not there
to snap ID

photos of dorsal fins
or back saddles, not there
to drop the pickle

that lets you listen in
on the precise language
distinct to this one clan,

this one tiny genetically distinct
transient pod of mammal-eating
killer whales that you watched,

carefully, for more than half
your life, a family
cut short by the spill,

pod quietly not
making babies,
as you did not

make babies though
you loved some fully,
impossible that their genes

like yours
will not live on,
though a new generation

will move in
to their hunting grounds, a new
set of predators

will eat what they can find,
and new teams
of scientists (some trained by you)

will watch, glassing the calm
water, or finding a snug
cove to wait out the worst

blows, the wind so cold
it hollows your bones, wind
you longed for

when you were too long
confined inside, cold cutting biting
wind that could kill you

but never did,
wind full of prayers, wind
that followed you

from Silver Creek to Prince William Sound
to Homer to Kapa'au, wind
that confuses even the seas,

air alive all over this earth, air
where you live, beloved become
earth, become water, become fire, become wind.

EVA'S CAIRN

On Valentine's Day we headed up to Kapa'au
to the land, land they planted with mango,
papaya, breadfruit, avocado, land they planted
with native hibiscus, o'hia, bamboo, grasses,
land of the year-round garden, land
wandered by shining chickens, cranky geese,
wild pigs, land sloping
down to the cliffside, up to the bluff
overlooking the ocean, trades whipping through,
lifting what's light enough,
carrying it off, bluff
where we gather
around a round flat basket of blossoms
orange yellow fuchsia white, gather
beside the cairn stacked up
to honor our friend,
the one whose beloved reads
one of her poems each morning
and weeps, drifting, missing
what he will never know of her, missing
every gesture of the woman
who brought to yoga a mat so filthy
it was all the teacher could see at first,
woman who was nervous
when she stood before a thousand people
to read with two world-renowned writers, woman
brilliant between them, woman who made a valentine
for her psychic friend who didn't see this coming,
valentine that taught her generosity
toward herself, woman who stopped
when she saw a white-haired man
bent in his garden, stopped
and asked if she could help
and when he said no, he didn't need
any help told him *she* needed to help,

could she? and for years
came to weed, to talk story, to harvest,
to sell at the open-air market
healthy organic vegetables
she helped bring into this world,
steadfast woman who mothered
and befriended Eve, Elli, Lars,
the one who missed them
the weeks they spent with their mom,
woman who delighted in being Omi
to Findlay and Sparrow, the future,
rascal woman who delighted in swearing,
the one who cussed her way
through the kneading
of a wide bowl of Latvian dough,
the patient one who all her life attended
to this earth, who watched and waited even
when whales did not appear, woman
who tended to killer whales though she knew their lives
remain mostly mystery, tended
to this earth's creatures, all of us, woman who took in
a troubled boy and tended him, turned
his life toward life though her own life
she already knew was not renewing
and so she turned
toward death until she could say
death is inky, death is cold, death
is beyond fear, death
is perfect,

her husband slow
to let go
his need
to restore her, their life,
his responsibility to keep things

running, things she knew
were each moment a little farther
out of reach, woman who offered
grace in each good-bye, grace
in anger, grace in laughter,
grace in terror, grace in
clumsiness, grace in peace,
grace in weaving
everything she felt
into a basket casket of rituals, subtle
aroma of warm earth opening,
luna moth spiraling into the dark.

THE HOLINESS OF THE GROUND

The holiness of the ground returns
even when fire passes over. Even
when scorching eats up all the food.
Holiness feeds us, feeds
on us, holy. No matter
the poisons, overuse,
neglect, the ground worships
water and air. Each seed
finds its place, roots tender
as fine hairs. Each root
thickens as the ground's strength
rises through it. From lava rock
to finest dust, from rich black loam
to solid caliche,
the earth holds holy
cutbank and cliff, many layers
exposed, slot canyons of the soul.

THE PIE DANCE

for Findlay, Eve, Eivin, Sparrow

When vog lifts off Hualalai,
somewhere on the island
a boy not allowed sugar
is doing the pie dance,

spending every last ounce of
cuteness to charm or wheedle
one mouthful of cream whipped
nearly to butter, one mouthful

of the forbidden.
Through the porthole
on his boogie board
he spies a whorl

of yellow tangs, lifts
his shining face to yell,
"They're having a party!"
Wind musses his wild

white corona of curls,
the ocean alive for him
(parrotfish, wrasse)
in a new way

every time he pays
attention. When his mother
bewildered by grief
cried and cried

he ran to his father,
ran outside, ran
not because he was too little
to understand but

because somewhere
on the cellular level
his body knew
what language

could not contain—
that some things
in this world
even the ones who love

us most
cannot make better. Some
things in this world
will leave

and not come back,
will leave us
no matter how
we dance.

Then one morning
Findlay wakes, runs
to tell his mama,
"Omi's back!"

Stunned, she asks,
"Where?" and he tilts his head,
smiles his curious smile,
runs to play.

All afternoon as they cruise
the orchard, gathering mango,
avocado, papaya, one monarch floats
nearby, keeps them company.

STRONG ENOUGH

Strong enough
to climb backward up
the heaving ladder
on the stern of the six-pack
dolphin charter. Strong
enough to ignore the stretch
along the scar
marking where the sentinel
node once gathered first
radioactive dye headed for
the clean-up crew of
lymph nodes. Strong enough
to wait until Captain Trip calls,
"Okay, pool's open" before
slipping with just a tiny
splash into the sea
pocked with dorsal fins and
festooned with dolphin spume,
strong enough to calm
my tunnel of breath as
sunlight radiates through saltwater
and out of the depths first
two noses, then five, then dozens,
a wave of sleek passing. Strong
enough to turn sideways and find
face to my face a wild eye, curious,
at home in this element I'm visiting,
floating among clicks and chirps bouncing
off everything, even me, signals
strong enough to alert
the whole suspended host
to danger, strong
enough to let them know which way
feels best, strong enough
to keep close the ones who need

to be gathered near, strong enough
to signal who speaks
our language, who knows this terrain,
who's bad news, strong enough
to overcome the bite that left a white
starburst scar, strong enough to
swim with the pod though
this wound's visible
from far off, evidence that we're not always
strong enough, not always fast enough, not
always able to get out of the way of teeth
strong enough to tear off a part of our
perfectly good body, tear it
off, swallow it, and swim away,
stronger now for the nourishment
our flesh offers while we bleed, wide open
to millions of organisms
immediately at home in any
open sore, strong enough
in numbers to do away with us
though we swim hard away, swim
among those of our kind
who might for a moment protect us, swim
toward the shining globe
of a bait ball shimmering,
millions of tiny lives, swimming
as long as we're strong enough.

LIVES OF SHADOWS, LINGERING SCENT

After editing Eva's essays
her heart-shattering luminous essays
ready to live their lives in this world

she has departed, I cannot tell apart
the grief I feel for her hard living
and her dying, the grief I feel

because her cancer, clever, evolved
to outwit every treatment,
every ritual, every morsel of hope. I cannot

separate her cancer story
from my own, cancer I want
to fade like my shadow, like all

shadows when the sun tucks
behind mountains,
the sky glorious scarlet

swaths, gauzy clouds
tattered by wind. Her grief
and mine, married.

The desert in bloom—
palo verde's
canopies of yellow,

javelina-munched prickly pear
nubbed out, halos sprouting
atop saguaros, lemon trees

most fragrant at sunrise
and twilight, lemon scent
calling to every being

that can breathe—
yes, death's right here,
death lives among us.

This spring
Eva knew
she would not see,

her first spring
beyond us, makes room.
Lovely, the sunrise

caught in cholla blossoms,
the roadrunner's mad red
eye slash. Gone.

BECOMING EARTH

Death is perfect. —Eva Saulitis
Christmas Eve, 2015

From the molten core, lava pushes up
through Puʻu ʻŌʻō vent, sluices to the sea
becoming earth.

By listening, orcas single out one king salmon
among thousands of leaner pinks
becoming earth.

In disappearing birch forest
leaf and twig and bird nest fall
becoming earth.

At the root of King Tree where generations
let go, offerings fade, transform, ash & bone
becoming earth.

Swaddled in volcanic spume Hualalai
shudders, unpredictable, cracks
becoming earth.

Transplanted saguaro break caliche
sending roots through rock
becoming earth.

Flame touched to wick all over the world
this sacred smoke, breath
becoming earth.

Tucked into branches woven
for this purpose, Eva travels on
becoming earth.

Quiet inside, quiet out
the luna moth lifts, spirals, returns
becoming earth.

from

ESPERANZA'S HAIR

The leopard did not know, could not know, that he longed for love and cruelty and the hot pleasure of tearing things to pieces and the wind carrying the scent of a deer, but something suffocated and rebelled within him.

—Jorge Luis Borges (Inferno, I, 32)

ESPERANZA'S HAIR

Near the square in the dead part of town
the widow of the herbalist hums.
Still lovely, she tends him,
then scents her long hair.

She allowed the embalmer his ceremony,
but sent the bearers away.
The herbalist won't get out of his hammock.
He listens to her because her hands rub his feet.
He dreams of her hands, long and narrow
as a man's hands, bringing gunboats
of potatoes, spinach, shrimp
steaming to their table. He dreams of her hair
glued to her skin, after they use her body.

You sang, she says, wet my mouth,
numbed my nose and skin.
We have this beginning. I remember
you brought me canned goods, plates.
But you told me wrong.

I tried to get away. I packed my combs,
but the raft wouldn't hold.
The river took charge of my articles.

The grape-colored water stirs
small hosannas. I do not deny that this gift
of denial is a real gift. But the heat engines
in my body take special pains, like a sailor's letter.

So I wash my face under a corner lamp.
I twist my hair up for you. That's why.
I never thought there was a history to it.

A CRACK IN THE BALANCED SHIP

Since you wish to be on the balanced ship,
I shall not push you off. —Telemachus

Bored with the perfect geometry of four legs,
four walls, all the right angles,
a young wife lives for the third part of the night

after stars balance heat and this raw flesh age.
Thinking, she shakes the yoke:
marriage is salt, vital and basic;

mine, a salted mine
where promise catches light
but the miner comes home dirty.

Stroking the appalling softness below her belly
she splits into two sisters who can't stand to share
the same room. They agree to live on alternate days.

The river one, in love with casual water, sings,
What do you do with other men
after you promise a husband?

The earth one, watching stars row past,
crafts a balanced ship
and does not give way.

LANDLADY

Her face is deep gray,
spiderwebs drooped over handfuls of dirt

Twilight settles like a dog on the porch
with my textbook Spanish, her toothless grin

Talk of her children and the pain in her side
which returns each time they leave

News of the new grandson, healthy,
plans for a garden

Then her rough spotted hand
like a wing on my knee

proudly announcing *la boda bellísima,* her youngest niece
and a handsome mechanic, *con mariachis, un baile, y mucha comida*

then quiet, as her eyes travel down
her legs, two wide loaves of french bread

poking out beneath her skirt
and she whispers,

> *Mi hijita,* don't marry. Leave yourself time.
> Learn this: I am ugly inside from waiting.

PANCHO VILLA MEETS EL MUDO, THE DEAF SHOPKEEPER

Cananea, Mexico, 1910

Guns first, then beans,
and when the bins held only dust,
threats with the shoulder-fitted parts
of smuggled rifles.
In a good year, my father,
El Mudo, haggled in sign language
three pesos, take it or leave it
over a kilo of pintos heaped in their freckles
on the wide steel scoop.
But that year the only pods we split
grew high up, out of reach—
palo verde and mesquite,
frijoles indios. Our bellies
rose just a little that year,
tight round pouches of not enough.
Mother was glad she could not hear
the empty languages of stomachs.
God, she was lovely, even with
four kids and a dog.
When the raiders glanced around
for a ripe girl, they weren't sure
if her defect should protect her.
Then they saw my father
pushing under their mustaches
prize saddles, unstained bridles.
My hearing brother remembers they yelled
words he couldn't know, but he knew
were bad, so Dad threatened them
with the mysterious omniscience
of silence. He simply stood,
lifted his chest, and clenched
one fist at a time.
His long nightshirt split the black air
and they saw him there, part specter,

part saint, a still white smear
blasting their plans.
So they painted us a few nightmares—
tore into our mattresses,
broke all the plates. Ripped even
the one down comforter
kept for decoration on the bedstead
beside the baby's crate, and the baby
moved his mouth like a fish mouth
calling the white riot *beautiful,*
he didn't know any better. To him,
this was a game, spinning feathers
with his breath.
Yucca pointed the way, scattered
Villa's men, they
showed their knife blades
to my father, then swung right legs
over their horses.
David said it lasted long after
we couldn't see. Those horses' feet
made the sounds of hell, he said,
but I wouldn't know. All that time
my own feet cramped around the sack
my father had stuffed up under my hem.
America was in that sack.
I just didn't know it then.

PRAYING FOR SCARS

Along the Mogollon Rim
from Young to Payson
toppers lop the tips off ponderosa pine,
clearing the high-wired air.

Boots with teeth bite hard,
barking up a foothold.

Laid back tight in his
wide leather sling,
the new guy jerks twice,
pulleyed tense for his saw.

She rises to him, smiling,
chained partner still willing to flirt.
So high, pure air seduces.

The topper steadies his hips
and balances pressure, flak,
the tree's resistance. Half through,
the chain snags a fist of rock
knotted deep in the grain,
a stone lifted from under the earth
and levitated over the innocent years
of his coming up, agate shoved
as the sap rose each sticky season.

They were both out of place in the air.

The steel teeth spit, and the saw
bucked, a twister-arcing bronc
cracking branches backward,
splitting him that quick,
axe-head hard on a firm wedge,
split him clean as a seasoned rail.

Arm alone, cheap flap
of tissue and bone, first-aid bandana
limp. No better kiss to make it better.
The foreman tied him sitting up,
roped the loose arm fast
to his chilling side.
The ground was red before he got there.
Christmas trees lay slaughtered all around.
From every mouth, prayers for scars,
for something to show when he might tell this story,
prayers for the angry breath of proud flesh.

WELLDIGGER

A flame darts from his thumbnail, balances
on the match head. "*Fyrstikker,*" he says.
Folks don't think about fire anymore.

Lungs burning with ice, they dig wells by hand.
He shovels dirt into the pail, hollers for Erling
to draw it up. Snorts once, hard, like a horse,
spits gritty mucus.

Five body-lengths down he squints up
at the creaking, his hand against the glare.
Erling kicks a frozen spike of earth off the edge.
Below, the pick takes one step before it falls.

Erling calls, "Engebretson? Hey?" and Hannah comes out,
coarse flour powdering her hands like dirt.
Erl struggles him out of the hole. His hand is clamped over the wound
and puddles form in the hollows of his collarbones.

His stiff felt hat covers that dent
the rest of his life. But his children see
the fire, the wick of his body.

JIGSAW PUZZLES

Just inside the kitchen door
of the house on Calle Ileo
the old Maytag twisted against her hoses
like a half-broken mare.
We were kids then. We never paid much attention.
The red dish drainer,
cruddy from years of us
half learning to do chores
mildewed on top of the special cupboard.
Not the ragbag, where Mom hid bottles
when Grandpa Howe came through town.
And not the stretching place over the oven
where she stashed the Twinkies we couldn't afford.
But down here, skyscraper stacks
of jigsaw boxes, within reach,
almost all Midwestern farmhouses, barns, and fields,
flowerbeds tripping over themselves to get to the lakes.
Nothing like that around here. One thousand pieces,
interlocking. Wisconsin, in chunks
all over the table. For weeks
we'd eat standing up,
beans and wieners and instant potatoes
till the last piece fell in
and Mom's eye took on
that thick shine
and we barely breathed, no one even could
step into the room where it lay
finished, settled, clear.
She was saving it for him.
And when he came home
and took one look, mumbling, on the way
to the back bathroom, Mom started it
and we helped,
crumbling in three seconds
the corncribs, the silos, the fields gone

fallow. She'd talk in riddles
for a couple of days.
Nobody understood, but then
we were kids. We never paid much attention.

A DIVORCED MOTHER WITH CHILDREN

Hanna stands behind the planter box
denting an aluminum pan
on the cranium of her daughter.
The pansies stare,
their pug faces flat,
bewildered as that of Sing Ling
the crippled neighbor's commie dog
who digs through vegetable bins,
biting the purple onions of revenge.
Adobe flakes off under the nails
of the sullen girl scratching for balance.
Something breaks inside her mother,
something bigger than tantrums of embroidery,
boil your life down to that,
goddammit a turquoise Naugahyde
sectional sofa and these kids forever
popping out like varicose
don't lie to me,
shit-for-brains, how many times
I got to tell you—
don't go right from wearing diapers
to changing them.

THE APPLE

Mother slices

the apple

without sawing

twirls out

the blossom end

the seeds with

one crisp swipe. Cross-

sectioned womb,

one for me, one

for sister.

Mother with one

hand open

and one fist clenched.

THE LEVER BETWEEN HER BREASTS

1.

Dad slams the door. The floor feels cool.
We cut the feet off my pajamas.
I peek through the hole where the doorknob used to be.
Mom has her glasses off.

Mom makes Swiss steak. Dad is late.
We hear the Harley, see the smear of candy-apple red.
He asks everyone out for dinner and another drink.
Mom pours sauce and steak in the trash.

The Watsons break our window with a brick.
Go back to sleep.
Aunt Anna puts our hair in ponytails.
Mom is in a tent because she can't breathe.
Her medicine is all used up.

2.

After the divorce, Mom takes up smoking.
We don't have a box for the poor kids anymore.
Sue watches TV and sucks her thumb.
Ginny learns to fuck and drink. I walk down
drainage ditches. Mom is stark naked
on the rollaway bed. Her makeup's smeared,
her breasts.
I want to stab him, burn him
his pimpled butt leaves me helpless.

3.

Mrs. Palmer insists she is sleeping.
Mrs. Oliver brings chicken and fruit.

Mac touches her fingers till my uncles pry him away.
He was the last, the only name
out of two years of zippers and gin.
In my dream he says, "Breathe. Again. Harder."
She rips the lever between her breasts.
Chest gaping, she heaves that lever through the mirror.
I look at the corpse but the face keeps changing
into each of us who put her there.

CALVINISM

When the knob on my calf
reached the size of an egg,
my mother held a doubled-edged blade
in the blue-gas flame.
Look away when I lance it,
she did too so the putrid spray
hit only her earlobe and the left lens
of her glasses. I misheard her, *abscess,*
and pictured instead, in my leg,
the bottomless hole
sinners fall into, evil ones
cast into my leg and me
walking around with muscles full
of other folks' deceptions.
No wonder the teakettle screamed,
I did too, as the packs boiled away
layer after layer. My cooled skin
peeled away easily as bologna
once you find the edge.
Remind me to change the wick.
Every day accordion-pleated pressed gauze
tempted the poison out of the wound
until the morning the dressing came away
clean as it went on and I knew
about limbo, a dance involving a broomstick
and flesh bending back, and I knew about belief,
and the boiling oblivion.

from

THE CIRCLE OF TOTEMS

But blue will swallow black like a bell swallows silence "to echo a grief that is hardly human." Because blue contracts, retreats, it is the color of transcendence, leading us away in pursuit of the infinite.

—William Gass, *On Being Blue*

GLASS RATTLESNAKES AND THE THREE INCOMPARABLE DAUGHTERS OF MARISOL

That night the clouds gathered in packs,
Stray dogs napping, rolling in dirt.
Mimosas bent, gossiping, to the ground.

When her breathing came heavy,
Marisol moaned for her daughters.
The room was bare, except for a bowl
Filled with plain dirt, the kind
Growling outside anyone's window.

> *I had hoped to do better*
> *But this is all I have to leave you—*
> *One scoop each of common soil.*
>
> *Take it now, and choose*
> *Which life you'll let it give you.*

When the last words escaped her, slowly
Marisol opened her eyes on each of her daughters.
She felt a smooth coil loosen,
Releasing her heart.
Another slid down her spine,
Riding for pleasure that spiral
Waxed banister. The third was stingy,
Its rattles strongest, the third
Held on till she turned clay,
And only then gave up
Its corkscrew hold on her sex.

So it was that death came to her,
A simple woman who left nothing
But her last breath, some plain dirt,
And her name, Marisol.
The sea took the wavy part, mar.
The sun was left without a shadow, sol.

Marisol kept only the keening vowel, *eee*
The mean prayer of her leaving.
She opened her mouth.

Three braided glass rattlesnakes
Shimmied onto her tongue, balanced there
On the dried gourds of their tails.
Marisol tipped back her head,
One last glance at blue Venus,
And the snakes flipped off, cliff divers
Hanging on midair gasps, swooping,
Slicing, dazzling down,
Spangling her tiles with clear
Splintered fangs.

Alegría,
The oldest daughter, reached over
And closed her mother's eyes.
With the same hand, she mashed
Fistfuls of dirt into a wide red canoe.
She kissed her sisters, then slid
Three snake slivers under her sandal strap.
The moon pulled her canoe downstream
Past the oil slick of the estuary,
Past the what-if, what-if frog echoes,
Into the wallow of the Three Crocodiles.
She fed each beast a chunk of glass,
And the glass lit up the leathery skins,
Shining through the seams. So it was
That each part of her could see
Where it was going, through the jaws'
Gateways, deep into the tails' jungles,
Every part of her could see
The whole time they devoured her.

Tristeza,
The middle daughter, combed her mother's hair
And arranged the chilling limbs to resemble
A gentle mother, napping. Then she patted
A thick quilt from her share of the soil,
Spread it in honor over her mother.
The quilt was a comfort but didn't quite
Cover her cold left foot. Each stitch
Sprouted fruit trees—peaches, apricots,
Ruddy nectarines. Her orchard without fail
Gave back a harvest large as the appetite
Of the woman rumored to sleep under the mountain,
The restless one whose turning split the fields
And swallowed plowing farmers, their horses, their swearing.
Tristeza set up a stand at the edge of the highway,
A wooden ramada by the busy crossroads.
People stopped to ask her permission to
Glean the ripe hangers-on. They bit, teeth piercing
The downy skins, juices swimming across their tongues.
They ate in the cool shadows of the strange toes
Of rock stranded at the edge of the grove.
Tristeza fed them. They asked for more.

Deseo,
The baby, clamped the earth tight
And would not let go. She spit on her fist
And a jaguar was born. She fed it
Hot goat's milk, scratched its forever itching
Back. The jaguar began at her ankles,
Licked her calves, she wanted more,
Licked until she begged in Portuguese.
That jaguar would not do everything she wanted.
All night Deseo climbed the staircases of tequila,
No more, panting, *end here, steps, no more.*
She reached the top landing, the one with carpets

Playing up to the blue wall, carpets
Sagging over the trapdoor. Glass eyes. Sharp pupils.
The jaguar crouched beneath her skirt.
When she touched herself, anthills!
Anthills erupted everywhere she touched herself.

THE GARDEN OF EARTHLY DELIGHTS: DETAIL, TUCSON

That summer we swiped chunks of two-by-fours
heaped by the cracking slabs
poured for new houses
exactly like ours, more families settling
for the exact same carport, asphalt
so soft in August our kickstands
sank in, left pedals
digging their own graves
right where they fell.

Mice in the dog chow,
crankcase oil dripped
on the crisp deformed
larkspur, the few
clutching petals
hardy and doomed.

We traced petroglyphs
in the crusty manure.

Dad's '64 Harley, cherried.
This was before the Big One,
before Mom unjammed the junk drawer,
dug out the split-handled
ball-peen hammer and sank the rounded end
with cool precision *tank tank tank*
across the sexy
paint, till we could have set up
Chinese checkers.

Before, when the square gray barbecue
still had wheels. We heaved it
over the lip of the patio to wait
forever for the coals to burn down.

That Sunday, she came to the sliding door
just as Dad touched the match
to the fluid-soaked briquets—
                    whoosh and flare—
her face rippled and huge under glass.

THE WAITRESS'S KID

Before you left for the Lucky Strike,
I ironed your outfit—straight black
indestructible skirt, low-cut ruffles
on the K-Mart blouse. I hated

the chore as you must have the job—
toting beer to the leagues, Al Ball's
Chevron, Addressograph Multigraph.
Once, I made you late. You came

when I called, and held me,
fought for me against some pure
and adolescent pain. Most nights
we couldn't afford it.

You'd bring home the best
of a bad lot to dance till they fell,
the crashing bodies payment
against some larger debt.

I'd yell, then cry most school nights
till exhaustion tucked you in.
But one night my anger rose past
double-edged blades in the back bathroom,

and I uncapped the little white tube
free from the Avon Lady, Furious Passion,
my color, not yours, and wrote in virgin lipstick
three words on the mirror, then opened the window

and left. You held your lipstick smack
against your mouth, one wide pull
in each direction. You'd smear your lips
against each other, then kiss

a square of toilet paper, leaving always
surprised, a mouth. Under the oleanders
behind the public pool, I waited
for you to miss me. I knew you would yell

I know you can hear me just like you used to
when I was little and you said *stay*
within hollering distance or else, and you did
yell *I know you can*

hear me, but I heard in your voice how much
you did not know. When you left, desperate,
to wake up my friends, I walked home up the arroyo,
sure the punishment would be swift.

FIRST THING IN THE MORNING, ÉCLAIRS, LIGHTNING

All night, the sky in frenzy.

Before the restless
town has stretched and
coughed, the baker's
dough has risen, browned,
cooled, then shaken
in perfect slices between steel
blades. All the delicious
emptinesses impaled with
custard or cream
present themselves on paper
doilies like second,
better thoughts.

His deft
palm pats sliced
almonds against
the sheer face
of a triple
rum cake.

Back home, his obese
dusty-eyed
daughter is calling
socorro, socorro, the walker
somehow through the flash-ripped
night has strayed
simpering in its rubber
shoes too far
from her
unsprung bed.

Almond, almond, almond—
in the whipped fragile
middle of a batch of royal
icing, he reads her lips.

He will have to leave work swearing
violently to tend her
because too much
how he loves
her, is too much.

SUGARBIRD, HIDING

The ferryboat's wake
has taken morning to St. Thomas.

Though her hair is short,
the woman left behind

shakes her head in the sun.
She hides now,

a sugarbird
liquid between leaves,

glides like oiled fingers
over the temples of her lover.

In the hanging gardens
she finds a likeness

of a self she once imagined—
Nike, balanced, one wing open,

bending to remove her sandal.
Tall ships slice the immediate water.

The tuned delicacy of the tendons
in her neck would tempt a guitarist

but no one listens now, no one
looks on as she loosens her clothing,

dropping each piece in a path behind her.
She breaks the clear mosaic of the water.

On her chest two rose windows harden,
a decent politeness,

a saying *hello*. A deaf man
once held her hand too long

then explained *I could hear your heartbeat*
in my palm. She swims face down,

her breath piped in,
singing underwater, humming

How much we have to forgive . . .
till the lace-grained sun insists

with a constant thud
at the back of the head

Come back, come . . .
In a secret life

you can never tell if you're happy.
In her room, at this moment

her husband and his sister
search her luggage.

They insist she come to dinner
with a pleasant face.

OWL/BEATING

When the headlights bored through
we saw differently, not more.
The glow between the saguaro's spines.
Quick glint—
unlikely moisture on the hardpan
jeep trail—yards down
we marked it, some living thing
murmuring in unreliable light.
Growing feathers
as we stepped
softly toward it.
Two cupped hands
full of terror,
even as we smoothed
the shirred edges, cooed echoes
to the gurgles of strangled
owl language. Brushed out
a hollow in the velvet
mesquite. Restored
the heart to its place,
nearer the sky.

CINCO DE MAYO

One hot chunk of melting asphalt, this block
roped off between the Phoenix Hilton
and the Museum of Science. One night unsnapped
to celebrate Cinco de Mayo,

who cares por qué, time to party, la gente
packed tight as candies in las piñatas,
streetgangers riding low, ese, vato,
clean prom kids movin' on, careful
not to sit in rented threads.

Xicanindio setting up, centerstage—
the cowbell's rich *donk!*
calls in the congas—
Jambo's palms stroke the taut skins
between kisses hello to las hijas.

Los viejitos turn las cumbias, spinning
twirled beer bottles, one leg between stockinged thighs,
tight skirt riding up, Carmen's hair
blue in the false light, the cuíca moaning
lover, Zarco milking the groaning skin,
sweet muscles, everyone's naked, especially
those with clothes on, like that woman lit up
aquí on the corner, dancing alone, her white
strapless barely hanging on, white skirt
whispering around her calves, then rising
higher, hija, as she whirls, fireworks
breaking the sky, focusing la fiesta
upside down on the retina
of the museum's walk-in eye,
y el borracho staggers to pee in the fountain,
throws a star, and a rock falls.

BLUE APPLES

Grandfather chose a name—
Lan Ping—

and laid out clean
bands of cloth

while she waded
ankle-deep

in yellow mud. When he called,
her hair swung

over melon-shells, a white boat,
clay horses, one shoe.

The high-necked dress
attended her, her thighs whispering

so privately she dared not
look up. A drizzle—

blue window-beads, chattering
over the organized wrongdoing

of the fuchsia
sweating on her nightstand.

He tightened thick bandages
toe to heel

then turned from her stare.
Taught her to paint not the leaves

but the spaces
between the leaves.

OCTOBER, SNOW

Quiet snow takes on
the shape of the black branch
that's taking on snow.

This low
along the horizon,
the sun

seems hurt,
glazes one birch in last light.
First ice

across the Chena edges out
until two sharpnesses
wound each other into binding.

Dry snow gives way
to the slightest urgings. One black seed
ticks through the crust.

THE CIRCLE OF TOTEMS

At Saxman, the totems slash down
through the mist, anchor themselves
deep in the Ketchikan muskeg
with one massive stomp
of each flat foot.
The ground, the people,
shiver, and look up.
                    The totems have chosen
this place, where alder and hemlock
crowd so thick a horse can't pass through,
so tight the thick-skinned she-bear
swiping at salmonberries
must shove her cubs with the backside
of one blunt-clawed paw.
                    The totems have chosen
this rock, where chum and sockeye
whip upstream in a creek crammed full—
more fish than water—a creek where
eagles and ravens squawk, both clans
gorging themselves against the lean times,
freshening mouths lately filled
by unread entrails
by the canneries' pilings.
                    The lowest mouth
on one tall pole clamps down on the wrist
of an anguished boy. He heads out on a morning
that's spitting at him, a fine drizzle
beading his eyelashes. Weaves down
at the lowest tide to hunt devilfish,
feeling already the slick circles against his tongue.
Chewy arms for seconds
coil in the cast iron stewpot.
He can tell from the sky
this will be a good day
for devilfish.

From the surface, bayside,
his eyes show him only himself,
wavering, squinting, hanging out
on a snag at the water's edge.
One branch cracks loose, so he
pokes around, jabbing into the mouths of stone
even this low tide covers. The branch
sings a thuck and scraping song,
hard bark against hard rock,
till the boy's arms grow heavy.
His stomach sings too now, an empty song,
and he sees in his mind the hand
of his mother, patting his shoulder,
loving him even when he brings her
nothing. He wades knee-high.

At first, it's the same story—
wood against stone under a loosening sky—
but on the third try, something
throws back his stick, a soft spitting out
of its splintering. Devilfish!
He reaches right down to grab its arm,
reaches back and down so he's bent
breathing hard, reaches far in,
fingers stretched and tickling—

            Then the whole world
                                    bites down!

For a moment he thinks this red-black cloud
is ink, squirted across his face
by the struggling one.

Only later does he claim it as pain,
his arm stuck in the frozen-hinged maw

of this stone-beast his fist and feet can't hurt.
He yanks and jimmies, tries relaxing
but feels only the distant spreading of his bones
traveling through his opening flesh.

When he remembers to breathe,
he takes the deepest breath he can remember.
As soon as it's in, it wants out,
forces itself as a rippling long scream
up the hillside, through rocks and thickets,
past the work sheds where two Tlingit carpenters
are jacking up the roof of the carver's barn.
That scream clears the fog and brings the people,
his whole village, down.
The strongest men
try with iron bars to break the face
of the great rock oyster.
But the water's coming home, as it does.
Up to his hips, his waist,
the boy knows this is his day,
straightens himself as much as he can.
He looks at his people,
at the eagle,
the raven,
the beaver-tail clan.
The water around his chest
lifts him a little and he sings
his own song, a song of red and black,
of salmon shimmering in their buttons,
a song of fur buried under a stake
at the beach so sand and water
can scrub it white, white fur
his mother will sew at the edges
of new moccasins,
the ones he will wear a long time
without any holes wearing through.

His people remember the song,
though it passed through the air
only once. They sing it
for the master carver who sharpens
his chisels and sets to work,
honoring the boy's spirit
with a five-ton trunk of cedar.
The carver's tools chant—

Remember, remember, remember.
Prepare, prepare, prepare.

from

WINGS MOIST FROM THE OTHER WORLD

ONCE YOU NAME IT

Once you name it grass,
    the new-mown
    aroma will see you through winter.

Once you name it
    hard durum wheat, it will feed
    the world.

Name it & you assume
    you can stop looking. Though *snow*
    shows only one facet
    of flake or storm or bank, *powder*
    one quality of the slope
    we're sliding down.

Once you name it Mozart, you expect it
    to save you.

Once you name it
    it's yours. You've claimed it.
    Now you must tend it, watch it grow
    into its name, then grow
    out of its name, come
    into its own.

Once you name it home, it will live in you
    no matter where you live
    no matter how you live
    as long as you live.

Once you name it enemy, you devote your life to it.

Once you name it friend, it will forgive you.

Once you name it love, you begin not to know.

Name it blood, & you see how you're related.
   It thickens, rich pudding
   after death, after birth.

Name it death & you step toward it, just
   as you did before it
   weighed down the tongue,
   melted like a wafer
   or a mouthful of snow.

Once you name it birth, you breathe
   first breath
   & cry, cry
   for the world you've left, harder
   cry for the world
   you've come to, wide
   awake, helpless, unclothed
   but for your cloak
   of blood, hungry
   to put it to your mouth,
   that whole world
   you've yet to name.

GRAVITY

The rigid baby wrapped in rags
is all tucked in. The child amputee

moans softly. The insulated rich
enforce a peculiar quiet,

shushing seismic rumbles
from distended bellies. One day

we will all of us yield
to the attraction of the earth,

the little plots we've left.
Sullied water

seeks its own level
far down and still.

The spirit without a vocabulary
shrieks into the night like patriots

welcomed home.
Somehow we never get around

to talking about it, the pull
to be the quickest draw,

the holster unsnapped always.
It's the code of the West,

stranger. If you're new
to these parts,

listen up. Manifest Destiny
just got an oil change.

We're aimed downhill,
ready to roll, all pumped up.

DECISIVE VICTORY

The way the black Lab races for the water
quick as the leash-clip snaps off his collar.

The way the tanager circles above sunbathers.
Jet Ski, the way the redhead's straight ponytail whips

as she spins donuts on the water, bucking
her own wake. My God, the way we show off

what we carry inside. Each grain of pollen
a medieval mace, a weapon against breath.

The way we gather our violence, so the explosion
comes across as involuntary. The long way

home. A child strapped to her wheelchair, the way
administrators who have never met her

find cost effective. Clipped grass,
rubble walk, the back way. Rhubarb

in the front yard, the way the inside of a shoe
worn too far wears down the foot,

the inflamed spot spreading, the weight
of our own steps too much to take.

WHITE FIGUREHEAD AT ISLA NEGRA

Neruda first saw her
cutting through mist, her face
guiding mast and crow's nest,
the infinite rigging
in need of repair.

Chopped up in dry dock, the ship sold
piece by piece, the figurehead locked
in a salt-battered freight house at the pier.
The evening he found her, the wharf lay deserted,
just light enough from the west to turn her

pure white, then gold, ash rose, gray. Neruda knelt
before the locked door, wanting her, whispering
through the keyhole

mango, sangre, mano, cara
mango, blood, hand, face
araña, huerfano, chiste, muerte
spider, orphan, silly joke, death.

Slowly, slowly he made love
to this woman made of wood, slowly
with his mouth he took her in
into himself, where she dances
yes today over his swells and breakers
through his squalls and still waters.

Her aroma of barnacles and split timber
never mellowed, even after years on land.
The soldiers who flooded the stone house
on Isla Negra took it with them,
forever on their hands. They crushed delicate
ears of seashells, smashed cities
of odd bottles, chipped

mosaics of fishes and tiled faces
of the sun. The figurehead floated
in a thousand splinters,
rode the rising
crest of the tortured river, forced
churning through the house.

And the water could not help behaving
like water. Held back, it broke out
more vicious than before, breaking down
the stone house on Isla Negra, stirring up
killing muds, the swamp of great sorrow.

Neruda died heartsick, hearing
helicopters drop flames on his nation's
dreams. Thousands of
mourners gathered like storm clouds.

The soldiers, muscles aching,
licked their lips, and tasted salt.

YOUNG BOY DANCING AT PLAYA LOS MUERTOS

Had he been naked
as he skipped
shivering
out of the waves
we would not have known
he was so poor.

But he was not
naked. He wore
around his hips
an exhausted
pair of cast-off
underwear,
gathered up at the hip,
secured
with the wire twist
from some tourist's
loaf of bread.

He shivered,
the edges of his lips
blue as the Virgin's veil,
Semana Santa, Holy Week, too early
really for perfect swimming.
Vendors hawked
Taxco silver, mangoes
on a stick, onyx seahorses
chiming, whole perch
skewered and seared.
His eyes swam after
the fish boy.

Timbales called out the guitarrón—
mariachis knocked Norteño beats
blanket to blanket up the beach.

The skinny one held on to his saggy
pants, elbowed close to sing along.
Someone else's fat papá lifted an eyebrow
in invitation, laughed, and together
man and boy danced a slick merengue,
flicked their hips ta-ta-ta,
swirled, one hand
suave against the belly,
the other a green rooster
kikiriki-ki
sunrise all day long!

The boy's whole body
told its truth—
he was not starving, no matter
what his ribs said. And his skin
could go ahead and offer the opinions
of its array of scars—no slash,
no welt, no still-healing burn
along his face, neck, shoulder
could talk louder
than the genius of his tiny
hips, those quick and playful
acts of God.

THE PROVIDER

for my father

Both arms around your waist I buried
my face in the cracked black
leather of your jacket. The throaty Harley
leaned too far, throttle
cranked, hot pavement chewing up
our foot pegs.
Any stray patch of gravel
suicide. Scabby saguaro
lurched by, lean and wounded,
never young. You loved

pure speed, that bike, and me,
though I had no way
to see it then.
I was fifteen, amazed
at my body and amazed
at you, all six foot six
shutting down with one look
whistles and hot talk
as we eased blinking
out of the desert
into the Beachcomber,
shut down everybody, then turned

for the first time to look at me
not as your elbow or toe,
there all the time, easy to bump,
but the woman me, the one so far away
I'd left
before you noticed
I could run.

My showing up
slowed you down, made you trade in
your tunes, your bike, your axe—

your life a down payment on mine.
We both got took.
You soured selling Chevys
and office machines. I took care
of the little kids.

Once, I brought a college friend
to your place. Your fourth wife
sang with you, "Bad, Bad, Leroy Brown"
and "One Note Samba,"
you clunking along on the clavinet,
those canned drums thumping
like tired pistons.

It was 10:30 in the morning.
A pitcher of salty dogs already
loosened your joints. We sat
on red velvet overstuff
still shrouded in double-duty plastic.
George Wallace, you said,
the only clear choice. I left.

Father, I am ashamed
how ashamed of you
I've always been when
I know so little
and that little
learned by leaving.

                    Your absence
has carved in me a place
that healed like a cactus shoe—
hard, fragile, secret—
the deepest gashes
shelter

for some bounding pack rat
or startled cactus wren.

HANNA ZOE

Mother, because you died
so often

when I was a child
I must go back there

to the crippled mesquite
with your eyes in it

to all the head-on crashes
that did not kill you

to the barbed wire and sand
of your voice, wheezing hard

Don't go too far. You left us
milk money in a can. We left you

under a stone
with no last name, unwilling

to burden you
in death

with your unbearable life.
Who were you then?

Who are you now?
Did you know your father

came to see me
on the night he died

came to my bed and held me,
told me he was going?

I had so much to ask
I forgot

to tell him
to touch your face

that way that made you stop
for a moment, in peace.

HUNTING SCORPIONS

The parents were both alive then,
no divorce,
so we spent cool November
hunting scorpions in the Rincons,

turning rocks with our sneaker toes, checking
with twisted off greasewood switches
first the darker upturned faces of stone,
then the sandy rock shallows. We whisked

fuzzy seedpods over the moistness,
hunting the striped or tan
little hook of poison
curled over. We'd scoop them up

into Dixie cups and walk them
level back to camp,
back to the circle of rock we'd set
hemming in paper plates and dry mesquite

that gave us back
our fingers, chilled to curls.
The scorpions would scramble
against steep daffodils

waxing the sides of the cup,
so we'd calm them with a glug
or two of beer. Once Gin
floated hers, damn near got stung

before it drowned. Mostly, we
squished the soppy cup between two
fire pit rocks, and watched.
Most of the beer left

in a huff. The scorpion
caught a clawhold on the seam
and clambered up.
                    For a moment, it wavered, twitching,

then the edge of the cup
clenched in on itself, petals
pressing back to the bulb,
the trapped one ticking inside.

DUST DEVIL

Tucson

On this dry earth, forgiveness glides
like a cloud shadow

passing over a desert school yard
erasing the ragged shade
thrown by the palm frond ramada—

the almost-moist kiss of coolness
on a day so hot
the tetherball hangs
sticky and soft
at the end of its rope.

The girl on the fringe for dodgeball
stops, raises her face
to the blessing of this tempered sun,

soothing, welcome, nearly wet
in a place where water's always holy.

The whole world's lifted
grain by grain, each point sharpened
then pointed here,
now.

Gritty wind picks up,
whipped wind whirls—
all the boys corral their faces
in the crooks of their elbows
all the girls squat on parched heels
holding skirts down to shield
slick calves from mean sand stings.

Dust lifts itself up to the sky.

The girl rinses her eyes,
blinking above the drinking fountain's
leaping arc, turns

and is chosen—blindfolded, she's
twirled, told *You're it*, then left
to stumble dizzy, hands outstretched

toward the sound of breathing
just out of reach, the child knowing
everyone else is running, everyone else can see . . .

The sun's back out. Her closed eyelids glow
red as veined petals
of tulips held to light, tulips
she swiped from the flickering altar
at the feet of the Virgin
Our Mother of Sorrows, forced

blossoms, waxy offerings
lifted from someone else's God
on a dare.

GRAVEYARD SHIFT
22ND & TUCSON BOULEVARD

Most nights, I liked the place
fine. No schedule, no calls, no
supervisor upping some unreal
quota of keystrokes.
All I had to do was scrub floors,
stock shelves, make a little
change. No sweat.

Circle K had some
arrangement—for stores
close to the railroad,
extra patrols.

It was slow. Two cops
rousted the wino with the purple
bandana, shoved him
hurtling across the tracks.

I checked the level
on the unleaded, shivering.
Thawed my fingers around a cup
so black I saw myself haloed
in a strange neon moon.

I thought of the girls, asleep.
Finally, we had our own place.
No matter what,
they couldn't answer the door unless
they knew the voice.
Wished I could call. I bent

for an armload of Kent and Pall Mall,
heard the front doors scrape. *Wipe your*
feet I hollered. Wasn't a regular. He
wandered over by the back. I bent

again, then straightened halfway,
my eye catching
movement by the register.

He was turned away. *Hey,*
you can't come back here.
It was the voice
I'd use on children, firm. He turned,
hefted a smooth, face-sized
river stone and chanted

I'll bash
your fucking
head in.

We stood like that, his face
bloated and shaking. His shirttail
out and ripped. *Take anything*
you want. Up, up, up
bent elbows, the stone rose
two-handed over his head,
then down
and down
and down.

WHY IRA PRATT COCKED HIS HEAD LIKE THAT

Twelve hours a day, six days a week.
Stamping out staves, cattle tanks,
strongboxes, silo sheeting. At first his brain
swelled, slamming all night the same
steel chants, his bones jamming, misaligned.
They bought real glass for the windows.

A dropped sheet four-by-eight sliced off two toes.
The straw boss didn't dock him.
He walked lighter, repaired his own shoe.
God preserve us from what we get used to.
They paid the improvement on the home place.

The knocking in his head slacked off, and he slept.
Couldn't startle him if you drove a buckboard
through the bed. He liked Amy saying that.
The day after Easter, he rose early,
checked the nest. Watched newly hatched robins
open their beaks. Then his hands began to sweat.

IRA PRATT'S CHARTS OF THE STARS

Open your eyes, Zoe.

Mars closes in tonight,
easing over by Aldebaran.
Don't be fooled—it's easy
to mistake them. Both glow red
but Mars stays steady.

Zoe, when I look at the night sky I think
of beings more lonely than we are,
of the ancients whose pictures we still see
up there, and the shepherds who needed them to be.

Remember when Scorpio went
to sting Orion? The archer's past
danger now, shooting his arrows west.
Or maybe the scorpion hides
over the earth's ledge,
past our vision's reach.

Libra has grown very dim,
hard to find. What we've agreed to see
may not show up this time.
But Libra's there. And it's healthy, Zoe,
to reserve love for what we can't be sure of.
Every turn of the earth
speaks a new good-bye.
The going on was never rare.
We just live here, now, through
small guilts and large longings—

and when we see, staring past the healed bone
still hurting in winter, when we
see what *is*, not what we've been told,

it's a shelter, Zoe, to stand under,
to understand, this seeing
this being
twice alive.

THREE NOTES FROM A WOODEN FLUTE

A moon with two points
cradles chill mist.
Where you are,
                    can you see it?

Moist starlight on new moss—
flannel blue, a melting
snow ridge.

I care for this birch bud
so tightly wrapped
in itself
it seems solid.

One passing shadow,
    a trickle at the root,
a hush of breath
    along the unclothed limb—

it will somehow know
    to open.

CREAMER'S FIELD

Half-gold leaves abandon the birch.
Very soon frost heaves will shuck
great curls of road off the ridge.
The earth will harden, even the air
turn stiff.

            This stubbled field of barley
very soon will pull down deep into itself
all witness of the season's planting,
harvest, grazing—even this

            gray light glinting across vast
swoops of geese—black from far off
but dappled closer, and the fragile, elegant
crooks of sandhill cranes, lifting, settling.

            Down rests where they rest, among
buffleheads and canvasbacks,
all those languages passing through
one clean morning's air.

GLACIER, CALVING

Kachemak Bay, Alaska

We picked through shoulder-high
wide-blade grasses, listening to the fading
snicker and he-yup of the trainer
posting a skittish foal. The massive
hooves of unshod Morgans turned the soil,
carved hollows to catch timothy seed,
grave half-moons to cradle rain.

A sweet-water stream emptied across rock beach
into Kachemak Bay. Across the way, glaciers
thrust splintered shale into black-shined
moraine, quick rivers charging inside them.
The bay caught the light, threw it back.

Something inside you let go.
You spoke of your father, who never learned to read,
grinding his teeth as you helped his hand
scrawl the letters of his painful name.
You told of the grandmother who wished you
never born, for fear you'd be like him. I held you.
That bitter river coursed.

At sunset we hiked to the rough lumber cabin.
Mud daubers under the eaves
dove for our faces, then banked
and soared over the unfenced field.
All night mosquitoes drilled through sleep—
each slap of little death
awake, and wet, and echoing.

EXIT GLACIER

When we got close enough
we could hear

rivers inside the ice
heaving splits

the groaning of a ledge
about to

calve. Strewn in the moraine
fresh moose sign—

tawny oblong pellets
breaking up

sharp black shale. In one breath
ice and air—

history, the record
of breaking—

prophecy, the warning
of what's yet to break

out from under
four stories

of bone-crushing turquoise
retreating.

MELT

Sun-warmed cedar planks—
        the scent of spruce and peeling birch—
                your mouth finds mine, we turn

from the porch rail
        to take this journey of tongues—
                a shiver of moisture

the natural spring
        rainwater under snow
                a shimmer in the hollow.

STRONG STARS

Mottled grouse peck up
gizzard stones
before the first snow—

seasons move on
as if the human heart were not
infinitely fragile.

The sow bear's stained snout lifts,
sniffs the wind, then bows
to claws raking in

stems, berries, rasping leaves.
A twelve-year-old, pleased, tells her aunt
I kissed a boy four times and my tooth

grew back in.
Beside the barrow ditch, the bandy-legged fox
bounds into finger-thin willow.

Strong stars surround the green
wash of the aurora, God's love, the moisture
of a woman's orgasm . . .

From here, we can see much farther
than we can walk.
We walk to the edges of our bodies.

THE RUN OF SILVERS

If, inside me,
his one cell swam among millions
as if it knew the way,
met the ripe star falling
through my thick clouded sky

then plunged in headlong
renouncing even the tail that allowed it
to make the swim,

then I will tell our new
daughter or son, the one
taking shape, taking over
inside and out
that one afternoon

a run of silvers surged
through Resurrection Bay,
such hurry toward death!
Their potent ballet—muscular
dazzling leaps in the blinding
sparkle of an air they can't breathe—

how they hovered
in blue air—angels, perhaps,
messengers surely

sent to nourish and teach
those of us who might listen . . .

They did not know where
they were going,
they simply found their way.

We did not catch our supper that day.
Glacial spray from the crashing falls
chilled our faces, cleared our eyes.

In never-ending daylight
sea otters rocked
belly up on the incoming
tide, swallowing whole
blue mussels
stone pounded
against their chests.

We never had touched each other
in quite such tender danger.

RAPT

Glazed aspen, low sun, snag branches
snowed over except
where eagles choose to rest.
One jangles her head—neck

feathers splay, troubled and wrung.
She sneezes, then preens
tucking white over brown
lifts off, weightless,

catching the perfect surge, kicking
back a burst of white off laden
boughs, skimming
low over the vast

open river, the last in Alaska, wide Chilkat
running warm in December. A choir
of her sisters swivels
to watch.

Whoom, whoom, she's fast along the surface,
the inner curve of her wings filling
with light. Feet first, talons
flick-snatch a flap of silver

from the river. She lifts and banks,
someone *screes.* Not five feet
from me, she lands, spreading
her catch lengthwise

along the branch. Her claws
pin it still gasping—
her sharp beak
punctures. Liquid bites, *chlap, chlap*

so close I hear them
drip, hear the wet rip
as fish muscle turns
into eagle. What's not eaten

shivers, ripples. Slippery entrails spill,
shimmer over the limb. Iced
cottonwoods creak. Grainy wind
lifts sun-sparked snow. She glances

my way
without concern, her yellow
eyes intent. I shake
my head and feel

what has been wind-torn
mend.

CLITORIS

Surely a man named it.

If a woman had chosen, we'd
have hawk tongue, pearl
of flame, olala berry,
suck nubbin, jujube
tsunami.

SHORT HISTORY OF ONE HOUR'S DESIRE

For the lips of the recording engineer
    moistening each other as the lights bubble up
For the drunken student's breath of cloves
For the staple guns of flamenco heels
For the foreskin slid back over a chewy mushroom
    of oblivion
For the lupus victim carried to her toilet
For the throb of destruction in the baby's temple
For the deaf cartoonist's nodding fist
For the hiker's last switchback before he froze
For the mask maker's wall of weathered skulls
For oiled springlets on an athlete's brow
For the Russian priest's daughter, her tangles and
    tangles, her hip-length hair
For the composer's fingers stroking
    the businesswoman's ankle
For eyes of the safety patrol who knows
    how hunger hollows bones first
For women skiing cross country to reach by moonlight
    a place to be naked
For flames centering fine Thai soup
For the singed waitress delivering fried cheese

For the language of touching after long absence
For chicken-scratch dancers under the tamaracks
For molas layering common cloth to brilliance
For the grandmother fading while we go at it raw
For clean incisions on polished clay—water spirit!
For the shapes of animals on our genitals
For the scab's child uncovering a mailbox rattlesnake
For the miracles tortillas wear on their faces
For the hole behind the net
    catching a cancerous neighbor's breath
For the murderer's first child, born retarded
For the little junkie whore who does not repent

For the racehorse pumped full of painkillers
For the vasectomized man who raises as his own
    his wife's last child
For the man who keeps three wives, and is faithful
    to them all
For the wife nearly ready to have children
For Japanese flags, blood on white tile, no children
For twin obese toddlers moaning for Twinkies
For two fingers sewn back to the drummer's hand
For the split decisions of young girls bathing
For the stonewalled wife aiming into concrete
For carpets unvacuumed since he moved out
For the millionaire kneeling to edge his lawn
For the husband grateful beyond questions
    for his wife's return
For the horror of prayers, answered and answered
For the charango, the cuíca, the Día de los Muertos
For shards of flowerpots later mistaken
For the clear-headed moment lust recedes
For musky, bone-shattering novelty
For hundred-year-old letters uncommitted to the flames
For all the juices we can suck from one another
For the history of one hour's desire

from

UNDERGROUND RIVERS

Estoy mirando, oyendo,
con la mitad del alma en el mar y la mitad del alma en la tierra
y con los dos mitades del alma
miro el mundo.

—Pablo Neruda, "Sexual Water"

I am here, watching, listening,
with half of my soul at sea and half of my soul on land,
and with both halves of my soul
I watch the world.

—translated by James Wright & Robert Bly

TOO SOON AFTER RAIN

(Sonoran Desert, where the dead are
said to cherish fragrances)

Too soon after rain blue woman
takes a step toward her mother
long gone, that memory an aroma

of cilantro gathered from
tree wells. *Sopa fideo*, no bother
so soon after rain. The woman

wants to recall her future. Not the one
she will live, but the dreamt other
long gone, a mother's legacy. This aroma:

a sweaty man, welcome,
pours his skyful of sorrow inside her
too soon. After rain, blue woman

walks, each footprint an omen
shaped in earth, of earth, the mother
not gone. Long memory, that aroma

of death sprouting. Dark humus
feeding us, feeding on us and all others.
Too soon. After rain blue woman's
long gone, like memory. Now, the aroma.

PANTANO WASH

We rode hard
our swaybacked
dreams, loosened pebbles
with hoofpicks,
sang the stickers
out of our palms, soles,
sang the bruised foot
out from between boulders,
our family heaped
like stones on our chests.

We gave to the first one
who asked
our breath—
the hiss of yucca
pushing out
leafshoots,
steamed oceanbeds of marrow,

the stars unfurled like fiddleheads,
our laughter the fine grain
of ironwood, streambed, eyelid,
songs our childhood
forbade us to sing
till now, till now

our tongues clacking
like palo verde beans
dropping between
dry fishhooks
splayed over the barrel's
firm skin, prickly
pear nipped
by the jazz-drunk javelina
we followed,
loping bareback,

till we could hunker down
in all our shady places,
tasting the moisture
two small stones under the tongue
returned to us.

SADDLED

Like us, Jeri Lou was too little to know
why the Kotex saddle tied to her stick horse
might cause trouble.

She galloped through unstained
meadows far greener than anything
she'd ever seen,

steeplechased sprinkler heads,
leapt free of leg braces
fitted by charity

doctors in fezzes, leapt
into pure sun, her world
beyond body, floor-length

gown of silver light,
oleander slippers, satin reins
loose in her hand . . .

A different kind of mother
might have laughed,
might have asked,

"Where's the saddlehorn?"
and Jeri Lou could have
said, "This one's English, mum,"

but no. Nostrils streaming Camel smoke,
Mrs. Watson yanked her in,
yelled at the rest of us *Go home.*

High in the fruitless mulberry, we
saw Jeri Lou burdened with blood.
Hers, ours, all miscarried.

When she came out,
her stick horse bareback,
tossed over one shoulder

as if she were a hobo
about to hop a freight,
she brought us a story

of fists inside us
where babies grow,
fists squeezing blood

from the moon.
We were pretty sure
Jeri Lou made it all up,

on account of her mom
never told
a story that good.

CHURNING

Long before she stood at the counter
of the cream station in a rubber apron,
skimmed up a sample for the centrifuge,
whirled it, and slipped in two drops of ruby oil,
set the points of the calipers
just so, careful as a snake
balancing an egg on its fangs,
delicate, the farmer watching
not that he didn't trust E.J.'s daughter
you understand but business
is business and butterfat
determines how many sacks
of flour and meal
go home in that wagon &
whether or not
a few yards will unwind
from the bolt of muslin, new
cloth for Easter, fresh skirt
for his wife's made-over
go-to-meeting dress
and the good part of the old skirt
whipped up into a waistcoat
for the baby, before that,
before prices quoted
let Harriet know
whose skinny cow
wouldn't make it through
another Dakota winter, and whose
skinny kids wouldn't have a baked potato
to bring to school, before all that
she had one big chore—
butter.

After her father milked
& set tall cans in the pantry,
it was her job
to scoop off
risen cream with a slotted spoon,
slip it into a half-gallon
Mason jar, and shake.
Forever. Shake steady,
shake long, shake
till her arms
fell off.
First she'd slosh
white water,
rapids foaming,
then watch storm clouds
thundering, then witness
the miraculous conception—
gold, arising
via her muscles, her
shaking, her will—
flecks to clumps to a solid chunk
new body luscious,
prepared to anoint
hot bread, huge farm bowls
of mashed potatoes,
legions of string beans.
Whatever the seven sisters,
their parents, and the hired hands
couldn't eat, she got to sell.
What did she save her pennies for?
Crank and a paddle—
              a mail-order churn.

MILK

Spoiled, his sisters whispered, spoiled
town girl who never learned
to milk, who snuggled down

under covers while John lit
the kitchen stove, then laced up
work boots and tramped to the barn.

Calm Norvella never needed
halter or stanchion. Eyes
closed, she sighed, relieved,

his chapped hands stripping
two strands at a time,
galvanized zings foaming.

And Harriet, new farm wife
stretching in bed,
massaged bag balm

into the just-seen planet
orbiting the milky way
of her gown, homemade

secret they could
keep only a little
while longer.

EASTER, GRAVE TENDING

Village of Moen, Norway

Just after milking, Hannah Loften
tied back her skirts and knelt
among the lettered stones,

seven generations in need
of her thick wrist twisting
nettles, scraping back

winter's scrim, her stiff bristles
scouring themselves to nubs
against chiseled names

shed by those held close in stories,
shed too by those forgotten.
Hannah Loften rinsed and weeded

till one clear star rose,
the churchyard's constellations
spiraling around her,

fading as dawn
lifted night from her eyes,
one star outshining

the great blazing arc
Viking longboats
steered by.

Stars bright at noon
just not given to us then.
Evenings she whipstitched

edges of openwork,
hardanger holes spaced
evenly as graves,

their beauty
outlining
what's no longer there.

HILLCLIMB

I can't remember anymore
my mother's laugh, can't
recall the exact sound,
only that
it was loud and harsh and lasted
forever, har-harring its crude
way across Johnny's
so everybody stopped
chewing, and with fries
poised one end coated
red, turned to look.

No container for that laugh,
no handkerchief, no
hand-thrown mug, no
galvanized bucket, no
rough-lumber shed, no
oleander churchyard, no
glass-stained sanctuary. No
shallow grave, no
arroyo, no secret ravine. No
bowl of mountains, no
wall-to-wall carpet, no
greasewood, ironwood,
palo verde, mesquite.

That laugh broke the sky,
blue white shatter light
burnt crack of one world lost
piercing laser of new worlds laid open
thunder cloud-heart backlit
dusty earth-heart wide open and bare.
That laugh with a touch of molasses,
touch of delight once innocent
red-brown rainwater gushing in gutterstreams

over ankles of little kids making up
songs in their own languages,
once clear as rain-drenched
air after heat so tight
the inner membranes of nose and throat
thinned to parchment, blood hieroglyphs
dancing, shadow puppets
jerked around behind the scrim.

Then the rush—
menses, nosebleed,
iron-salt taste of blood,
our own blood, hers
so close to the surface
the simple kind gesture
of stopping her
from stepping in the path
of a speeding Duster
left five deep blue prints.
And the unkind gestures
lingered, spread purple, yellow,
crushed side of windfall lemon
no one could salvage.

That blood, that frail surface
passed down till one day
in the desert against the backdrop
of screaming Greeves and Ducati, my
unfaithful father and his delinquent
buddies ripped up fragile slopes
steep enough to flip cycles backward.

I rooted for the hills,
not the hillclimbers. As my father
revved and revved, flailed against

and fell back from the lip
of the summit, my blood could not stay
inside one more moment. Down
my shirtfront, between my legs,
head back, down my throat,
ice held to the bridge of my nose, her
voice annoyed, saying
we should cauterize
and my visions of the tool, what tool?
what tool to burn on purpose
delicate places we want to be tougher
and how could it help
hellfire aimed toward the brain
help to cool blood flooding
the lusty slapstick of blood
undammed and breathless
the throat exposed,
hard swallows, the high drama
of dailiness, the great gulps
of blood laughs
that hurt to hear, to see.

Nobody could survive such laughter.
She didn't. Neither did I. We both
died, one to the other, as she drifted
far beyond where any hand could reach her
and I grew into the woman
her bruises, her laughter
guaranteed I'd be.

OWLS' COUGH BALLS

Snake season—we bushwhack
sneezing past bobbling quail

start the unoiled windmill whir of
Inca doves

feigning wounds to draw us past
chicks and nest.

Globemallow, pinkeye bush,
childhood legends, lesions,

fears grown up with us—don't touch—stay
other, safe, apart. Mummy Mountain,

steep hillside named for the wrapped
and embalmed, the body hot

in its sarcophagus, graven
images outside of the idealized

ruler, divine, not guessing.
The soul sure for once—

this earth dances, palo verde
delirious yellow dances

blue-banded lizards skitter, waxy purple
petals on the prickly pear

samba their brief lives in splendor
then make way for ripe fruit.

Ocotillo for its cool day tangos
lush, abundant

stiff leaves secure
among thorns,

graceful droop of the sexual
blossoms, flamboyant

for their moment, this morning.
Foxtails' fine plum brushes

stroke, poke through to bare skin
skin still harboring

early morning chill of the snake nest,
coyote den, the burrows

of ground squirrels, the refuge
all creatures born of this earth

return to. Abandoned
radio spires

pick up signals
beyond our ken. Wiry

perches for three harbingers
among the spatters—screech owls

cough up
what they can't digest—

minute molars, half a skull,
femur and pelvis

mashed together, mangled,
matted among clumps

of rodents' coats
of many colors

dried fur binding
this new body, matter

immobile but filled
with stories,

lush,
left over.

AJO LILY

Two feet deep
under quartz and silica

under earth no path
marks off

the bulbs swell,
sweetness too deep

to lure larvae,
ground too hard

even wet years
to tempt claws.

Impossibly delicate
one layered shoot reaches up

pushing aside
massive rubble

rearranging the mosaic
of surface pebbles

so these clear blue bells
might echo

ajo, ajo,
the sky's voice

moments before
first drops bruise

dry earth,
before first drops

bead jojoba pods
where the swallowtail

drinks, moments before
a new shoot

slips slick as garlic
into a world deep blue

slit by sheet lightning,
pounded by hard water

insistent that we give
what we have

only ourselves
to feed all the world's hungry.

NIGHT-BLOOMING JASMINE

No, even though
his touch unfurls

the frowsy camellia's lack of restraint,
soothes the cool profusion of

slick-leafed calla lilies,
thumbs the tangled

tumble of honeysuckle, even so
I do not

love the man
beside me tonight.

The candles I know
by name,

the sesame oil's
skin-warmed aroma,

that second-hand moon.
Light sloshes bare skin.

Awkward thigh-step till toes touch
wood in the Japanese tub,

I try to set anchor,
ghost ship off shore.

Wild raccoons venture
out of the canyon, rest

an hour under the evening star
perched on the fence post—

inland lighthouse guiding
wayward birds of paradise.

This moment slips
incognito into

small waves
breaking away

from our bodies, waves
spilling starlight

over the tub's rim,
starlight we step in.

Our reflections
break, waver.

There is no love
in the world

absent
from this moment.

WHAT TO COUNT ON

Not one star, not even the half moon
            on the night you were born
Not the flash of salmon
            nor ridges on blue snow
Not the flicker of raven's
            never-still eye
Not breath frozen in fine hairs
            beading the bull moose's nostril
Not one hand under flannel
            warming before reaching
Not burbot at home under Tanana ice
            not burbot pulled up into failing light
Not the knife blade honed, not the leather sheath
Not raw bawling in the dog yard
            when the musher barks *gee*
Not the gnawed ends of wrist-thick sticks
            mounded over beaver dens
Not solar flares scouring the earth over China
Not rime crystals bearding a sleek cheek of snow
Not six minutes more of darkness each day
Not air water food words touch
Not art
Not anything we expect
Not anything we expect to keep
Not anything we expect to keep us alive

Not the center of the sea
Not the birthplace of the waves
Not the compass too close to true north to guide us

Then with no warning
            flukes of three orcas
                        rise, arc clear of sea water

RIME

Overnight, each twig has grown
white fur, the air so still
snow throws
into sharp relief each
branch plus
each branch's crooked
light-bent sense
of self, crystalized.
Last night, your voice
roused my limbs,
warm under flannel,
licked each branch,
split, and hollow,
licked into flame the untamed
liquids, flammable, spilled
down your chin,
moisture from the heart-
wood, risen unseasonably,
springing free not just from me,
nor your snow-cloud
juices just from you,
no—these waters
rise from the hot springs
at the center of the sacred,
from the little stone
overlooked, often,
plain little stone
where vibrations from each life
ever lived, each life
yet to be, gather.

THE STORY OF LIGHT

Think of the woman who first touched fire
to a hollow stone filled with seal oil,
how she fiddled with fuel and flame
until blue shadows before and after her
filled her house, crowded
the underground, then
fled like sky-captains
chasing the aurora's whale tail
green beyond the earth's curve.
Her tenth summer, the elders let her
raise her *issum,* seal pup orphaned
when hunters brought in her mother,
their grins of plenty
broad, red. The women
slit the hard belly.
Plopped among the ruby innards
steaming on rough-cut planks
blinked a new sea-child
whose first sound
came out a question
in the old language, a question
that in one throaty bark
asked *who,* meaning What family
is this? What comfort
do you provide for guests?
Do you let strangers remain
strangers? The women rinsed the slick pup
in cool water, crafted a pouch
for her to suck. Then the young girl
whose hands held light
even when the room did not
brought this new being
beside her bed, let it scatter
babiche and split birch
gathered for snowshoes, let it

nose the caribou neck hairs
bearding her dance fans. They
held up the fans to their foreheads,
playing white hair, playing old.
In the time when women do not sew
the seal danced at her first potlatch.
And when the lamps burned down
no one could see
any difference between waves
in rock, waves in sea.
The pup lifted her nose, licked
salt from seven stars, and slipped
light back among silvers and chum
light among ghostly belugas
swimming far north to offer themselves.

BEAR PLAN, BROOKS RANGE

Groggy in the half-life
just before sleep

snug up against you, limbs
pruned by the narrow bunk,

I jostle this first night
rowdy in the sleeping cabin

gnawed by porcupines. I murmur
over the murmur of a new hatch—

mosquitoes flocking black net
nailed neatly about our bunk,

murmur one question
asking not so much for an answer

but reassurance beyond your calm
drowsy scent naked and safe.

What's our bear plan?
Han jolts awake—*Bear plan?*

We have a bear plan? This afternoon
after bumping over the dotted line

at the Arctic Circle, after
yelling out at first sight,

jubilant, *There she is,*
the Mighty Yukon, after

landing the Widgeon
belly first, skimming the undisturbed

surface of Walker Lake,
propwash skittering

frantic pellets over Plexiglas,
we yawned to clear

full ears, pulled on
hipwaders, ferried our few days'

supplies to shore. Something big
had been here,

big enough, say,
to rip away both boat shed

doors, to leave hinges
bent into question marks

or snapped, metal
jagged as the Arrigetch, peaks

broken, heaved, slammed
into being.

Hanna found the footprints,
pigeon-toed, along the shore,

claw to heel half again longer
than her oversized sneakers,

wider than her amazed face.
We cache our food far

from where we'll sleep, cook
and wash up away

from where we'll spread
our bedrolls. What's

our bear plan? Joe, the one
among us born and raised here, says,

Make a lot of noise.
First time here, Han says,

That's it? Then Joe admits
he's brought a gun.

In the plane. And we picture it, fifty yards
down the beach,

across the bear path,
floating in thigh-high

ice water, picture too
our diaper waddle

swaddled in waders, and know
just how tenuous is

our brief time here.
One by one we drop off,

exhausted by possibilities,
wake to cub tracks

criss-crossing the tabula rasa
at the water's edge,

marvel at billows
of white butterflies

feeding on delicacies
we can't even see,

hollow black earth
turned in the night

by great curved claws
of ones watching

who do not allow themselves
to be seen.

AUBADE: MORNING AURORA

Dawn aurora churning
this morning
whole sky
a bright ether dream
the pink-tinged green
just before consciousness
fades . . .

This morning
your surgeon
holds in her capable hands
the tough purple fist
of your womb, the two nubbly
walnuts on their stalks,
ashes, ashes . . .

When you wake,
parched,
no water allowed,
lick your lips,
sigh through them
a single breath
the one the lights can hear, the one
that brings the sky
within reach . . .

So many legends
about the lights—
that just the right
whistle might lure
them down, that
wherever they touch
ground, blood
must follow . . .

Picture your healed self
            astride Orion,
blizzard stallion
            shying from ash in wind
shying from bare-limbed birch.

CAMOUFLAGE

Night dive, Kona

We've been told
not to kneel
even if sandy
paths between

outcrops of lava
look inviting.
That's where
crocodile eels

disappear.
And anything
that will let you
touch it,

don't. This I remember
unsteady in deep water
reaching to brace
one hand

and several tons of gear—
then I see, quick
& terrifying as any epiphany—
the rock's eyes

steady on me.
Titan scorpionfish.
This ambush
hunter, original

still life, suspends
time. My eyes trace
the great square jaw,
each stripe of fin, the toxic

spines flattened
to blend with red algae.
Vital disguise, his life
depends upon being mistaken

for stone. And mine,
at this moment upon being
not more than one breath
from my buddy,

shaking his dive light,
trying to catch my eye.
Who are we down here,
out of reach

of usual language?
Translating every gesture
of beings better adapted
to be here,

we suck our finite air
some of us calm as parrotfish
wrapped for the night in
self-made cocoons

some of us skittish
as red-speckled
octopi, remaking our shapes
each moment, each breath.

DIVE

Above, a quilt of molten glass,
the surface of time
liquid, each breath
suspended, rising
in capsules, CO_2
gleaned from our blood

Below, desire to know
how soft corals open themselves
to night, how parrotfish
sleep in slick cocoons
how shape-shifters escape,
eight arms through any exit
impossibly tiny, jagged, close

Below human need, invisible
trails of sound echo
whale to whale,
echo through oceans of time

Below the surface,
barnacled keels, dwarf
volcanoes sharp as lava
below the cinched Zodiac,
the archer, the target,
the zen letting go
below arrows of barracuda
whole quivers
shot

Below hard surge
bashing lava loose
below violet damselfish
below gold lace
nudibranchs coupling

below the betrayal of sabertooth
blennies posing
as cleaner wrasse, then
biting

Below wrecks of commerce
or war, wrecks of pleasure
sunk into sand
below artificial reefs
laid in brine, heated
by lava flows, hatched in air—

the eternal weather
of ocean inside us.

EACH RISE, EACH HOLLOW

You have taken me to a place
where ripe papaya let go their stems
and fell, heavy with juice, in our hands

You have taken me
fifty feet under, swimming
with eagle rays, while
humpbacks above us
sang their way south

You have shown me the ancient madrona
healed over barbed wire
nailed decades ago to red bark

You have held me shivering
before a flaring
crosshatch of split oak

In a small plane you have lifted me
over the San Juans,
all of us citizens of the clouds

You have taken me to a house
with windows to the sky,
walls open to night

You have made me your home

You have taken me to the place
mist barely conceals the next island,
where each rise, each hollow
opens, sacred

WHAT WILL REMAIN

Lit from inside, birches
spark, flare

blaze trails
for travelers

outstretched in air.
Tawny cranes

return to rest
where earth cradles water.

Cranes graze, pace, graze, then
flap scuttle jabber scold . . .

This harvest
flashes—wingspan of sand,

hillside of crooknecks
soon to move on.

What will remain
has always remained—

water seized
by ice-driven air,

faith through hard cold
that the languages

of marsh, sky,
sandhill crane

will keep on
with us or without.

from

BLAZE

THE TREES WON'T NOTICE

Trees have their own lives,
branching out each season
to catch and release

light—pure light or light
sifted through smoke, the edges
gorgeous, the burning forest.

The trees won't notice
how they touch us,
how our whole world

is named for one turn—
universe—cosmic laughter
raining steady

till the river rises.
To the painter
standing half a brush-length

away, this canvas becomes
the world, ridges of true
red crashing into violet

devastating and creating
continent, basin, range.
The messy precision

of making
love in all its glory
and beaver dam confusion

purposeful, passionate,
a matter of survival
each chewed trunk

living, then giving
life beyond its own
verso, recto

leaves turning,
the place where bark's
peeled back

complexion freshly scrubbed
the deliberate smear
layer upon layer

laid down wet
as the free and unmerited favor
of . . . well, maybe god

maybe the edge
of the not-yet
imagined

maybe the force
of the made thing.

AN INTIMACY

Falling
    and already
        fallen

May snow
    lights
        on tufts of moss

dusting
    the bizarre
        upholstery

springing from
    juts and crannies
        broken edges

where the birches'
    many-layered bodies
        have split, scrolled back

and left wide open
    the unblemished
        inner self.

A tinge
    of light-washed pink
        draws one to touch

the translucent ear
    of an infant,
        the open thighs

of a happy woman
    walking
        naked.

MATISSE'S ANTOINETTE

Because they are truly her friends, they leave her
tasting salt in her dreams, salt and green lemons.
Cool porcelain, a windowsill, vanilla, and wax.
                    Her friends leave her
flowers, and tied to the flowers, a note
scratched on butcher paper. Blue-black gentian
folded in a green waxed cone. Their last
cut hours sweated out formally, each stem
arranged in the swirl-glazed tureen.

In the bath, she stretches full-length—
two bruised red peonies surface.
Because she did not love him, she allowed
one young man to stroke the sleek slope
of her hip, wondering what he would find
to possess, what she had
to parcel, what one needs
must conserve, always. How little
it has to do with the body.

ELEGY FOR GETZ

Rough tongue, wet reed, a working girl's heel
lithe blood, nude bricks, a sorcerer's creel

A cantaloupe's grin as flesh slips from the shell
A ditch digger's *bossa*, the *favela*'s smells

A samba's raw onion sliced into threes
A mouthful of light released on the sea

Dirt road, raw skin, the ocean on fire
Curved claw, spiked toad, cool lizard desire

The torturer's daughter, the disappeared's shoe
Fresh bruises that throb, it's the blood, it's the blood

Old tracks, black beans, the birth water's gush
Chipped tooth, hot nails, a bolt of *cachaça*

A tongue touch of sweat on a bare collarbone
Red dance of that horse, a slingshot stone

Bright horn, brief life, brass tunnel of scars
Each breath, cracked seed, blown pollen of stars

WALKER LAKE

The sow bear ripped
down the boat tarp,
scraped black fur

into twisted wingnuts,
that bear
eased her itch and disappeared.

And still she stayed near,
while we hiked
uphill to fill our jug,

the spring covered over
with autumn's leavings.
We skimmed clear

frosted growth floating,
sank our jerrycans,
felt them pull deeper.

The surface healed
around wrists
stiff with cold.

Bubbles shook free
from river weeds, rose up,
tumbled downstream.

The still place returned
to reflection. Birch
startled us with gold

so loud our bodies
flared like fireweed
gone to seed.

Twilight
put its slant
on the afternoon—

four loons
swam near
our seaplane,

nudging this
strange relative
who would not speak.

The moon had eaten itself
down to the rind,
and in that sliver,

that lingering
of autumn, stars borrowed
the voices of loons.

JUST THIS ONCE

Everyone else snores.
Black nets billow, let in

a few mosquitoes.
I sneak out,

careful to prop shut
the cabin door so porcupines

won't be tempted, pull on
hipwaders folded knee-high,

head up the path
not singing,

not calling out, not
jangling bells

to warn the one who left
tracks bigger than ours

at the edge of the water
and her spring cub

who dawdled behind, clawing up
storm clouds of silt—

undisturbed and not disturbing
I stand still breathing in

sphagnum's mossy sigh
quiet after loon calls, follow

unmarked paths
left by stars too wild

to show themselves anywhere
but here, inhale

her nursing musk,
the bear

I know
is there.

THE TOLD SECRET

A young woman tells a secret, which she has promised
never to reveal. But slyly, so no one might accuse
her of telling, and no one can be sure it was she
who told. So now she has two secrets—the one
she has betrayed, and the fact of her treason.
Over the years, the weights of these intimacies
settle in her knees, which groan and creak and
remind her with a whole repertoire of pains the depths
of her duplicity. Because she cannot move, she gains
a reputation for stability. Troubled people
seek her out, people with unspeakable difficulties.
They confide in her relentlessly, each secret adding
its own specific weight to her body until even
her eyelids can no longer support themselves.
When she has absolutely room for no more, she hands
back an old confidence in exchange for each new one,
a trading of guilt across generations.
The old people's grievous embarrassments
the young take home as party favors.
Early on, this secret woman discovers that Truth in fact
is the greatest lie, so she always and immediately tells
what she sees. Everyone finds her insanely amusing.
In her later years she is much in demand
at dinner parties. One evening
a young woman does not laugh, though
everyone else in the room leans for balance
on the slim arms of potted palms. The old woman
draws the girl away, into the tiled kitchen.
Listen, I have something to tell you.

ANNIVERSARY

What being nests
in our hollows?

What being nests
in our broken places?

Bound, one self
rising into two

who year after year
stick around
stay

Testament, new
each morning, each day

What whorl
borne of both of us

peels loose?
What world

borne of both of us
lifts away?

GOD GESTURES

The hill disappears a little
each hour.

Birch leaves
break more light every day.

Next week, promise,
fresh salmon & stories,

laughter's holy communion.
In a month,

will we recognize
the one inside us?

Before long,
stones won't mind

claiming us,
kindred particles

of matter rushing
madder inside

able with word, song,
touch to offer

god gestures—
Ah, in you I feel

what will remain
when all else

memory body breath
has gone along.

SWANS, WHERE WE DON'T EXPECT THEM

Tundra swans twine necks
among snowflakes
vanishing into evening's

river. Past breakup,
tablecloths of rotten ice
nest along the bank.

Halfway, swan wings
open, then settle in
like second thoughts.

Maybe they flew
north over Minto,
traced halos

over brooding ponds,
saw from far up
without touching

the world is hard
and will stay hard
a while longer.

WIDE ICY RIVER

How, driving in whiteout
    above tree line, the summit
        road washed white, blue white
            gone to swirling powder, we gasp
                whirling inside the frosted sigh

of the earth.
    Straining in whiteout
        our eyes the eyes of creatures
            unsuited to this element
                vestigial, liquid ornaments

splashing for flashes of orange.
    Each marker hovers,
        flicks past too
            fast, we can't let it go, we can't
                see it or the next—

beyond our tiny sphere, the expanse—
    white on white, the endless
        domes of our unknowing.
            Our knowing
                what we cannot see

could very well whisk away
    our visible breath.

How the ones we loved
    well enough
        or not
            would miss us with a white-hot
                burning for as long as they

held on. And those who
held old photographs
would conjure our voices
above tree line, in whiteout,
the road drifted over.

Long after the photos
have fallen, white
flakes of ash
in a stranger's grate,
our distant, white-boned

daughter will warm her cold
ear along the thigh of her lover.
Her breath on his skin
white language
he can lose himself in

that white
on white
remake us
windswept blue
in its own image.

THE LONGEST NIGHT OF THE YEAR

Before contact, dancers around here
wore masks, carved parts of trees
into faces that revealed
what their own
covered up.

After days, after
long nights drumming,
chanting, raising hands, raising
voices to the sky,
dancers turned
their second faces
back to the earth,
left them to weather.
That whole day lit
only by gauzy green
aurora, the boreal
forest holding
still under snow.
Unmarked, the path
of the sun
among stars.

A century later, birch trees
mark a turning point—
more light every day
after this day.
A century later, birch trees
carve solstice riddles.

What face should we put on
for ceremonies? What face
should we wear every day?

With the sun so far away
how do we know
where to turn?

With our roots well covered,
our branches bare,
what are we?

Every night a face returns
to earth. Every morning
a new face is born.
What are we?

The answers
paper birch bark
whispers.

In stillness
paper birch bark peels.

from

GNAWED BONES

GNAWED BONES

If language is bones, hard parts
of speech, what do skulls of pack rats
crushed into owl pellets
have to tell us?

If this delicate pelvis
once balanced a gravid
javelina, what word passes on
to her shoats?

If cicada shells hang on
like single mothers starved
for touch, what does hot
wind whisper through them?

If every day
reenacts creation,
if we live
here, now

in the first world
and the last,
let us speak
in our bones

languages of water
from all skies, from
deep underground.
Let our bones quench

the thirst of history,
thirst for all we yearn
to sip, marrow
of each dry tongue.

NESTS, AN ELEGY

In a few seasons,
willows will reinvade

this burn,
slender red shoots

prime browse.
Even scorched

earth provides.
This burn

the size of Phoenix
didn't touch

a single
human house.

But migrants
nest here,

some returning
from Tierra

del Fuego
to this choking

land of fire,
their memories

tribal, alive
in every cell.

They come back,
the goldeneyes

forced to abandon
this year's pale green

clutch in the hollow
just catching.

Buffleheads flare higher,
their nests tinder

twenty feet up.
The marsh hawk's

bowl of dead reeds,
rock ptarmigan's

grass and moss,
the snowy owl's

lichens and feathers
exposed on bare tundra,

the ruffed grouse's
depression lined with leaves,

the great horned owl's
open surface, charred,

the falcon cleared out,
peregrine along

rivers of smoke, blind
but rising, ashes rising.

AS WAR GOES ON

for Phil, Hari, Drew
& all makers of symbolic paper
www.ivaw.org

Olive trees do not apologize.
Dusty, their uniforms
drop piece by piece

splattering the sidewalk.
No one can eat such fruit
without curing it in lye.

Brine. Oceans. Eyes.
Overflowing. Paper
beaten from sweat-

stained camouflage
shed by men ready
to be seen,

to speak. From the fountain
fresh waters. Vets beat
to a pulp

loosened fibers,
spread onto screens
the mash of their lives.

Soldiers so young
they've yet to bear
fruit, veterans

so old their roots
tangle, tap
rivers underground.

On the paper
we make of our lives
what shall we write?

DESERT ODYSSEY

Like us, Telemachus didn't know
where to start
when father didn't come home.

Face down in a field, his mouth
split by stones,
he might need us. We spread out,

hit Tucson Bowl, the Beachcomber,
the Maverick,
listening for his whiskery line

trolling for barflies, pickled
laughter, amber waves—
grain siphoned from bottomless kegs.

TOUCH AND GO

Gone to pick up two dozen
hot from the deep fat
chocolate-frosted,
custard, coconut, cake,

and his favorite, raised and glazed,
he pays cash, swoops up the box
each sweet straight and level
gliding under the lid's window.

Takeoffs and landings . . .
he makes room on the seat,
moving aside the body
he's built, Styrofoam,

engine embedded, taped, wings
detached. At the four-way
stop, his head spirals,
stress cracks, splits.

Nose down breaks the stall
and you'll fly again . . .
He guns it while he
can see, flies low

by trailers, saguaro,
his last turn home,
eases down so smooth
he and the plane are one—

fuel off, flying as long as—
he scans for his spot, swallows
two tablets he's heard
can help when blood's

not getting where it needs
to go and blood
rushes free, floods
all emergency

landing strips, old dirt
roads, dry fields,
any flat patch
where he might put down.

YOU'RE HERE

He closes
his huge hand over hers,
drawing her close.

"I've been alone four days."
He's confined
behind rails,

in a bed that lifts
feet or head but not
his heart, sure now

that if he knew then
what he knows now
he'd never have come

never have let her call
never have left
his chair where

he realized how completely
something'd gone
wrong, chair where

he was last himself, chair
where he'll never
settle again. "Four days,"

he says. "By myself."
"I know," she says, "but
I'm here now." Tired

woman who has not left
his side, woman
unshowered, stiff

from dropping off
in the bedside chair,
woman who knows

he's right, her man
who mistook her
for his mother

late in the night,
child again in the dark
alone her husband

who's been somewhere
she can't go
with him,

husband headed somewhere
she can't go
with him, husband.

SWALLOWS

That moment not dusk but just before—

The earth turned away a bit more
from the sun, last shadows not long
for this land. Our steps disturbed
tiny winged creatures who risked
their lives to fly ankle high
late glimmers rising so
sleek fork-tailed
swoop-winged swallows
whipped through, snicked up
beak after beak full of ticking.

Those moments inside us we don't for years
comprehend, until the morning
miles away when we pretend
it's important to spoon into a helpless elder
a little peach yogurt and he pretends
clean now after a kind Ukrainian
stranger has bathed him in bed
that swallowing whatever's on the held spoon
might be how he'd choose to spend
the last moments left him.

He swallows twice the strained
yogurt, twice sips of honey-thick
nectar, then spits the straw,
bright-eyed. *I'll swallow*
three times if I want to. Grins.
Swallows for good
every last word.
Those moments hand in hand,
his eyes on mine, when what he utters
I can't understand.

Swallows. Twice. Again.

HA HA HA

More than once before you had fooled us, taken time off
from breathing, a showman's pause drawn out
longer than was wise, longer than the crowd could bear

then taken us all in with that ragged
rasp, what the lung man called Cheyne-Stokes,
a pattern of leaving and returning

then huffing hard to make up
for whatever you left behind
all those years. Your chest stayed still.

Your hand in my hand, warm
still. Your eyes a color I'd not seen
closed as if finally

you had escaped and no one ever
again could hold you
responsible, your last joke.

NO SIGN

One generation passeth away,
and another generation cometh. —Ecclesiastes 1:4

Just moments after your death,
a young woman, very young, knocks
then peeks

around the hospital door
I'd closed.
"I clean now?" She smiles,

ready to make our world
better. I blurt,
"My father has died."

Deep wells, her eyes,
water she doesn't hide.
"Mi padre también."

And we're in each other's
worlds right then, in each other's
arms, found in this translation.

Perky, used to coaxing
half-conscious or deeply ill
folks without appetites,

the dietician
breezes in.
"Ready to choose

your dinner,
Mister . . ."
. . . And then she sees.

His wife's daughters arrive,
take their turns
kissing his forehead,

the only father
they've known
lo these many years.

Then two strapping
young men swagger in,
snapping on latex gloves

and start to touch him.
"Why are you here?" I whisper.
"To turn him,"

they declare, confident,
reaching. "You're aware
my father has died?"

Both recoil
as if they hadn't suspected
such a thing existed

within their realm,
back out
filling the still air

with their young
men's stuttered
apologies.

BEYOND WORDS, THIS LANGUAGE

The morning I was born
                    you held my hand.

The morning you died
                    I held your hand.

What's left
                    to forgive?

ALBÓNDIGAS

In clear broth
among bits of rice
float little worlds

rolled between
her palms,
globes spiced

with cominos, ajo,
cilantro, cebolla,
simmered

in fresh caldo
for us this time
albóndigas

just the way
he liked it,
my father

who just months
before his death
hit us up for a loan

we could have his pension
all he wanted was
a motorhome

he figured out
they just didn't fit—
Incompatible!

so could we work something out
he had to get out
he'd like to get

out on the road
just find a spot
where he could play

a few tunes, tell a few jokes,
have a drink
when he felt like it . . .

We didn't float him
the loan. We offered a place
he could take some time.

Two weeks later
he gassed up his car, drove home,
gassed up hers like always.

She can't stand to pull up
to the pump, she tells us,
can't stand that smell.

He always did that
my sweet baby
that was his job

she says, glancing
up at the glass
top of the curio

cabinet, her eyes
lingering, the dark
blue velvet bag

shrouding the box
holding the few
heavy bits she has left.

WHEN GROUND CANNOT TAKE IN MORE RAIN

Downhill from rare
pines twisted

as sorrow's logic,
the estuary

shines, blocked
but for one bridged river,

turning back on itself
tide by tide.

Those clouds were once
this water on our faces.

Across the moon those clouds
have no doubts. Jostled

by every breeze, every whisper
those clouds have somewhere

to get to, even if
their rain falls

but fails
to reach earth.

Even if
the earth

cannot take in
what they must give.

LAND FRAUD NOSEBLEED

We'd be out in the desert
fifteen miles from Fort Huachuca
checking out the latest

bogus development—street
signs tilting in *caliche*,
no water, no electricity,

just salesmen yapping
like freshly groomed poodles
and my strapped parents nodding

nodding but never talking,
never signing, just polite
till the Mexican cooks

opened the pit
and FREE BBQ smoke
watered our eyes and mouths.

Right then, on cue,
my mother would glance over
just as my nose flooded,

blots big as summer raindrops
staining my crop top and shorts,
and the salesmen running up

with Dixie cups of crushed
ice, almost heaven
if I didn't hold it

too long
to the bridge
of my nose . . .

Then plates of shredded
beef and pinto beans, green
chiles and white bread

appeared like mirages—
plenty, enough, too much
so we ate

what we could,
said thanks, really,
foiled the rest

and balanced
paper plates on
bare knees

all the way, tissues
mashed to my tilted-back
face, getting away

with it,
all the way
home.

Saguaros tied up
in surveyor's tape,
cacti packing heat,

held their own seeds
hostage on high,
Apache tears packed buckshot tight.

The cracker box trailer-office got
hauled off to the next patch
of creosote and jumping cactus.

The dirt stayed. Trash
hung around, blew off
with dust devils, snagged

on barbed wire. Before the heat
of the day, uprooted Yaqui
women whose third language

tasted metallic,
sharp blades of English
on the tongue, rose,

lifted saguaro ribs
and ocotillo spikes
to whap down

fruit out of reach.
They picked up those strong enough
not to split,

left behind those broken,
bleeding
into a new generation.

GO TO THE BROOM CLOSET AND PICK OUT A STICK

Fish sticks and french fries.
Beans and wieners and instant
potatoes. Red goop. Gray goop.
Don't tell me Mom couldn't cook.
Allemande left with your left hand.
With her glasses off, Mom never heard
a word we said. She had us
convinced. She could see
through walls, around
corners. She could hear
what we were thinking.
We were afraid
she could see our secrets
even from her grave.
Make the world
go away,
get it ah-off
my sho-ol-der.
Mirror lost, she couldn't signal.
Ladies Center Back to the Bar.
Hinge and Flutter. Flare the Star.
Off-key, she rasped
from the depths of her sinuses
songs, spelunkers.
Swing your partner,
right and left grand.
Raw gash, Grand Canyon the same age
as geological loneliness, her
bones. Ancient oceans.
Slot canyons twisted
inside her,
worn down
by what ran through.
What do I know of her loneliness?

ASTHMA

The reason she couldn't swim, couldn't
push us on swings.
The reason we moved away
from the sea into the desert.
The reason one whole cupboard rattled with her pills.
The reason palo verde in bloom
sent her careening to St. Joe's. The reason I sat close,
grabbed the wheel when her lips turned blue.
The reason she hugged so hard.
The reason no animal found refuge in her lap.
The reason she stashed
vodka bottles in the ragbag.
The reason she yelled,
"Go to the broom closet and pick out
a stick." The reason smoke
filled her eyes. The reason
mournful cowboy songs riddled her.
The reason her first breaths
in the morning scraped and clattered
like rusty hay balers.

The reason she couldn't carry a tune
in a bushel basket with a lid.
The reason she sang anyway.
The reason at sunset in her throat her husband
kick-started his Harley, spit gravel behind him
as he peeled out. The reason her laugh—sheet lightning—
cracked the sky. The reason she picked through
spaghetti she didn't make herself.
The reason she quit eating.
The reason she loved quiet
more than her own kids. The reason quiet never entered her
body, never entered her mind. The reason she didn't want to
be here. The reason she left. The reason we buried her
under a stone with no last name.

SKY OF SOULS

Trembling at the edges, the night sky's
not wide enough—northern lights
breeze beyond rolling horizons,

scalloped hills, the simple
curve of our earth.
A soul learns nothing

while a soul. The deepest spirals
baptize our eyes in lights,
dip into the beautiful black

mouth of mystery. And the souls
feel it, the not-knowing
they cannot bear, they love

questions so much.
A holy man
once told me

a child can atone
for her mother's death
wish. Beneath these soul-spiked

lights I believe
he might be right.
I shall atone

each time I breathe
these lights,
each time I listen

to beings I cannot see,
each time I open myself
trembling

at the edges,
lighting the whole wide
whirling sky.

MOTHER TONGUE

In a language recently
disappeared, god
is talking.

No one knows anymore
how long the leaves
keep silent

how deep
the stones' truth
lies buried

what silent kinship
glints off blond fur
where grizzly cubs graze.

In the far time, nearly
everyone could speak
with salmon,

water,
clouds, stars.
Every body.

Now no one sees the ocean
though it lives in every tear.

In a language lost to us
god is singing.

DELIVERANCE

after Chagall

What kind of Moses
would arrive in the form
of a rooster tall enough

to brush his comb
along the doorjamb,
his arched back

a feathered saddle,
iridescent, not with sweat?
One roll of his red eye

and this unrepentant woman
mounts up, clings to wattle
and tendon, leans her ear to his beak

to catch each triangular
syllable tremulous as dawn.
Her doubts burrow

deep into down, she strokes
veins at the base of his throat,
feels the faint tick of faith

just out of reach.
The silty creek of her mind
cannot yet float

that rowboat where some tiny god's
giving one of the chosen
a free ride to the other side.

IN PRAISE, EPHEMERA

At dawn feeding swans, upended
by the ice shelf, black beaks
champing half-thawed weeds,

draw us to the riverbank. Grizzled feathers,
echo of boots over rotting snow. Far between,
few, tundra swans step out on late ice.

Glacial melt, snow melt
hustle downstream—
ice dams hold tight

jostled swathes of half-lace ice.
Knife-edged narrow
leads open, sliced river swollen.

Muskrat and beaver gnaw
new shoots of red willow,
open winter lodges. Fresh water, air.

Pollen, lavish, carpets the
quick and the dead, blessing the
revived, blessing the remade.

Season of cold broken. Season of ice broken. Season of
tattered shirtsleeves. Bare hands
useful again after burrowing all winter.

Voles gather first shoots of new grasses,
weave fresh sheaves to put by, chew new roots, shoots, and
xylem, drunk on the season's sugars risen

yesterday and today, this hour
zipping by, lifting off, wild swan in clear sky.

OATMEAL

Dry slide of Bob's Red Mill
Extra Thick Rolled Oats
off the scoop—

tiny dustcloud
settling like ash
from stirred coals.

Waking together,
happy, not
our first try.

KUS-SUN-AR

For an injured friend,
he brings salmon fillets, fish
he caught dipnetting all night at Chitina.
Needle-nose pliers nipped out
all the invisible bones.

Growing up at fish camp, he'd sneeze.
Elders said, "Kus-sun-ar."
Otter. They invoked otter's name
to wish him close
to one who lives in more than one world.
Shaman helper, on land, in water.

He tells me otters live inside women, curled up
just above the stomach,
and this feels true. I feel my otters,
restless, disturbed.

My hurt body can't rest yet,
it was so close to the other world.

I'm an otter, skinned in the round,
my pelt pulled off in one piece.
Stitched into a kit bag,
I feel the shaman
feeding me salmon,
placing his healing
tools one by one
into my emptiness.

SPLEEN

Who needs angels?
I have avenging nieces,
who have taken biology

and believe true justice
compels them
to track down

the kid screaming illegally
down the bike path,
four-wheel ATV blind

behind brush,
split seconds before
he tossed our lives like dice.

The avenging nieces reason
it's only fair—
a spleen for a spleen—

They're pretty sure
once they've got him
open, they can pick his out

and once removed
seal it in a Mason jar,
unvented for posterity.

NAMING WHAT WE HOLD IN OUR HANDS

Penny.
Paperclip.

Key.
Rubber band.

So far
the signals

from fingertips
to brain

to lips,
wild leaps

electrical
chemical.

What could be
more simple?

Until the day
we cannot

do it.
What then

do we hold
in our hand?

Secret lives
unspoken

names
of everyday

things. The doctor
of missed connections

waits.
The least injured

part of me
wants to look him

straight in the soul
and identify

by touch alone
what our hands hold:

shooting star
red aurora

mist forest
life after this.

Life.

CHATANIKA

High, the Chatanika,
high this year, surges
the flats, soaks
the valley. Chatanika

spreads wide
where gravel braids.
Where banks
snug close,

where rock,
earth, and root
gang up, high water
scours, carves,

its own image
changeable.
Chatanika, in pools
deep green, in eddies

steeped tea, freezes
and thaws, makes its way on,
full of grayling
flashing like thoughts

among the millions
of mirrors at Minto.
What brought me
exactly here?

Is my flowing
through the world
a fit gift? Have I nourished
more roots than I undercut?

LONG BEFORE WE GOT HERE, LONG AFTER WE'RE GONE

In the season blue-white sun
barely lifts above the ridge,
limps along the horizon
then dives out of sight,
we're changed each day by light.

Someone who's gone before
broke trail, set tracks.
With the right kick wax,
we make our way among birch
breathing hard rare frosted light.

We make of light arpeggio crystals,
caribou dance fans, shush
of bristles. One moment made
alive, human, unafraid.
All that's lost not gone.

from

TOUCAN NEST

GENESIS, QUETZAL

Swallow at dawn one
tiny avocado. Hold so still
the world begins.

Love cry
of the jaguar dyes
crimson

your deepest belly
down. Each glance a
hummingbird, preening,

the narrow trail
of her open bill.
Amethyst geode

throat, copper-green
wing. Blink once
and stars take flight—

sing like trogons, motmots,
yellow-thighed finches, sooty
robins, nightingale thrushes,

acorn *carpinteros*
tucked into carved-out holes,
wrens and siskins

seen or hidden.
Cataratas, water-
falls of song. Your chest,

vest of drip tips,
highland forest awake
after rain. Breeze-

ruffled streams,
your tails
run to the Pacific,

waves hungry
to mingle
with reef and sand,

velvet green crest,
teal of tide pool.
When you push off,

flowerpiercers and
flycatchers fall
from your feathers.

When you push off,
earth gasps and sighs.
Your wings stir

root aromas tangled
underfoot. When you push off,
cloud and sky

reshape around you.
When you push off,
a new world spins.

BLUE-GRAY TANAGER, HERE, GONE

Pájaro I've pictured
floats, toes open

toward
her perch—

wings backlit
gold-white

ripe color
forty years gone—

my mother,
her hair.

Our dead
appear

vanish.
So much

we can't know.
So we spend

our lives
asking.

Kind. Joyful and kind,
he remembers, distant

cousin who knew
her young, poised

for flight
into a sky

cool as the blue
aroma of gardenia

not yet crushed.
Elfin, light—clean brook—

in her path
each root, rock, rough

edge freshens.
Her hair,

white-blonde
halo, fine

as dandelion
fluff. Wave

gathering foam
about to crest.

He knew her.
Remembers

my mother
graceful

before
four kids

before she turned
twenty-four.

KEEPING LOUD ONES QUIET

"You love macaws, right?
My great-aunt
has a scarlet macaw,
her best friend."

Eloise hesitates,
doesn't say, "I'd like to strangle
your great-aunt."
"Here's the deal," she says.

That cherished pet, wings
clipped, neurotic,
pampered with sleigh bells and plastic
globes whirling

has for twenty years
heard no voice
from her flock, seen
no feather except

in mirrors. She's never
flown, though she still
stretches cut wings
through her dreams.

For this confined life
a hundred birds died,
hatchlings poached
from borderline nests

wet forest, dry forest,
park and preserve.
Packed in wheel wells,
in false-bottomed vans,

in car doors and camper
shells, in crates
and cages, drugged
to keep them quiet . . .

In shock, in disguise
as boots or masks,
stuffed into jacket
pockets, wings banded

they flew, baggage
undeclared. They bumped
dusty over gravel
byways. Some arrived

breathing, panicky,
revived in Tokyo, London,
Paris, Newark,
LA, Oaxaca,

Des Moines.
Lucky, *los loros*
left to the sky.
Not so the thousands

caged and admired
the hundreds
of thousands
plucked or dumped.

What we love
we hold close.
We bring to our eyes
expensive glass,

draw what's wild into heart
and mind. Celebrate this moment
on the wing, twenty macaws,
scarlet flock squawking.

SLOTH

Thirty feet up, even
slower than we thought, honey-
blonde three-toed

perezosa
spans the great Y
between branches. Arced

claws unfold, cutlery
close at hand.
She hangs wide

open, a great gold X
crossing paths with
the bloodied man

thorn-torn in cathedrals.
Her tongue dangles
moist leaves.

Foot over hand, her
gradual shifts
sculpt

time.
She's at home
in dense fur.

We groundlings
suffer dripping
coats of salt.

Why should
her pace
suggest sin?

Her quizzical
face, placid
as faith

that one day
visions might catch up
to endless questions.

TOUCAN NEST

Cautious as a stalked ex,
chestnut mandibled toucan

profiled in a far triangle
makes sure no one's tailing her . . .

then shoves off. Quick
flight, *te dé, te dé,*

toward lofty hollows.
The tree swallows

her great curved face, yellow
bib, red belly, dainty

blue legs. Inside the tree
nest shrieks of hunger.

Within the living
trunk, true shelter

of decay. She cracks
her bill to spill

half-digested
fruits and lizards

down yawning
gullets,

cramming four
unfeathered young.

It's her secret
tucked tree deep

how she turns in there,
emerges

tip first,
half of her

that gleaming bill
serrated yellow

spliced brown,
dangling shreds

she shows her throat
to swallow.

HOW THE MOTMOT GOT THAT TAIL

When Sibo asked
every creature to help
make the world,

the motmot
hid
in a hole.

All the other animals,
all the other birds,
did their share.

A tattler saw
the motmot's tail,
plucked out one feather

then another. All the birds
chipped in, plucked.
Tired out just before they finished.

When the world was complete,
Sibo gave the birds a rest.
Motmot showed up, bragged

I did more than
all of you put together!
But his tail

testified.
He could not hide
his lazy behind.

VENOM

The gardener
bashes in

the gorgeous
triangular head

of the *fer-de-lance,*
most venomous

víbora he knows.
Ay! One bite

and you're dead.
His forked stick

lifts looped,
lank snake,

draped away
from his legs.

I ask to look—
slithers to earth

spoiled coil
turned clay.

Hermosa, I sigh.
Mosaic

scales, cream,
black, brown.

He nods.
Hermosa y

peligrosa. Muy
peligrosa.

Our guide
conjures prayers,

apologies.
The forked stick

slings pure danger
behind the shed.

BASILISK LIZARD

for William Kloefkorn

Lusty jitterbug
amplified by
corrugated rust

scares the bejesus
out of us. Before
roof flakes

settle, freckle
rust-earth
tiles, you skitter

toward water. Your toes
hinge over, longer
than your feet.

Little king, named
for a made-up
mess, part rooster,

part dragon, part
snake, you're very much awake
cooling your tail in the pool,

lifting, alert,
to every footfall,
wingbeat, breath.

With a single glance,
the story goes,
the basilisk

could stop
a heart. One step
too close

and you're
panic incarnate—
Jesus Christ

Lizard zipping
zigzag on hind legs,
kicking up

trails of rain,
salvation's *sip sip*
sip into mist.

GETTING AWAY

We sidewind inside clouds
along ridgelines dividing
waters that shed east
from waters that shed west—

el páramo, which I know
only from Pedro, the Páramo
from Comala, hometown so hot
dead folks arriving in Hell

go back to get their blankets.
In the Talamancas, rufous-
naped sparrows shove mashed-up
worms beak to beak.

We glide down, down, toward
the Tárcoles River, where
twenty crocs per kilometer
make their ancient living

except here, at the bridge,
where dozens of huge ones
snap and shove, chomp down
junk that people throw.

Around the bend, spoonbills,
rosy and plump, strain
rivermuck. By treadless tires
wood storks hunker, shoulders hunched.

Quick plovers and stilts
pace cuneiform messages.
Green herons call, call
downriver, then follow

their voices. Lone
royal egret paces very near
two half-submerged
relics plastered in mud.

They're sharp toothed, zap
fast, *fuerte*. But she
can lift
up out of silt and soar.

PAINTED CART WITH NO OXEN

Legend has it that in ancestral
forest under a waning moon
church carpenters cut
bitter cedar for a new altar,

bitter cedar for new saints.
They stacked chopped logs
outside their workshop,
curled into their hammocks.

That fingernail of light
let the stars shine brighter.
Two former altar boys
crept up, rolled the logs

into the river. They rode them
the long way home.
When the wood dried,
they built a shelter

for their mother, a table,
a bench, and then
crafted an oxcart sturdier
than anyone had ever seen.

On it their sister painted
curls, feathers,
their mother's favorite flowers,
triangles in all colors,

silk threads and broad swaths,
every color joy owns,
colors of macaw, volcano,
epiphyte, ocean foam.

Priests warned from the pulpit
that coffee plants
would bear no cherries,
that fish would slip out

of mended nets,
that milk cows would
go dry, and chickens
stop laying—all this

and roasting in Hell
would befall
whoever had stolen
the sacred wood.

But the former altar boys
knew from older stories
that the roots of the
bitter cedar speak

through their branches
to the stars. And the stars,
brighter tonight, heard
their prayers, their thanks

for shelter, for a table,
for a cart of many colors
that they hauled themselves
bringing in their mother's harvest,

their crippled neighbor's
harvest, more coffee
than ever, hauled without help
to a town downstream.

San José,
a carpenter too, watched
all this from on high.
He liked the spirit

of these brothers in wood.
He sent them on a detour
on the way home, past
a farm where twin oxen

had just been born. They traded
the promise of hauling
for the newborns, loaded them
onto fresh leaves in the *cajón,*

pulled with their own muscles
in the last light of the stars,
pulled twin oxen in the painted cart
back to their fields, back home.

TENT REVIVAL

If after
afternoon rains
you hang
under a blue tarp
this worn bedsheet,

then position
behind it a lamp
& before it a bench,
all manner of visitors
will descend.

Most wish you no harm.
Invertebrates smaller
than the nail
on an infant's little finger
tremble, backlit

beside luna moths
wide as masks
feathered for carnival.
Mosaic in motion,
triangles of tent-wings.

Tatted, bobbin spun,
hardanger, crewel work—
the delicacy and strength
of lace. Sepia ink
on hand-laid paper,

openwork cut
with manicure scissors.
One magnificent
jeweled fellow—
cloisonné patterns

red-brown and tan—
twirls antennae
twice his length,
draws the world
to him, to him, to him.

Dripping still,
water flows over us,
carves fresh paths
down the mountain,
& underground.

Strangers here,
we draw this world
to us, to us, to us,
world we've just begun
to sense, to take in.

BURNT FIELDS

Panicked iguanas hustle,
rough-winged swallows
sky-skitter,
víboras in furrows

slither when farmers
on purpose
to rid cane of razors
set fire to ripe fields.

Choking clouds of flamed
sugar billow,
balloon. Three soot-streaked men
machete-whack stalks,

sweat dripping
as if they're melting.
Sharp edges—
skin's cut

right through wet shirts.
Crosshatched scars
one shade lighter
track hard muscles.

Fangs men's sharp eyes
watch for
wait, coils
of poison. Costly

sweetness, smudged.
Rice and beans
this sugar buys,
schoolbooks, *zapatos*.

Tongue touch
of pleasure—
in *café con leche,*
in shots of *guaro*

at *el baile en Sábado.*
Man-high grass hacked
to stubble—scorched
cane thrown haystack high—

stragglers overflowing
wood slat & wire wagons,
grimy old tractor straining
uphill to the crusher, up to the mill.

STRANGLER FIG

Cousins, then,
the myriad orchids
of the mist forest
and this towering
strangler fig.

Both start
tenuous life
as stowaways
tossed aside
by wind or wing

dropped
without anyone's
noticing
high above
the forest floor.

Air plants,
epiphytes, bromeliads
plastered so heavy
some branches
crack, tumble.

But the fig's patient.
It settles in,
sucks what it can
from leaf rot, from
breaks in bark,

drinks deep
from fine mist.
Then into air
fig tentacles
unfurl, aiming

toward the host's
small patch of soil.
Fig leaves above
cover all else.
Not out of modesty.

Each fig takes its own
special wasp
to carry on,
wasp that swaps
pollen for protection.

Nearly gone,
the host lingers
within the fig
like the memory
of a difficult parent

who never knew
what she was taking on
when she got you,
mother who resented
being tied down,

mother whose face
you can't quite
picture, mother
who changed so much
those last years

you barely knew her,
broken mother
asthmatic, wheezy,
who gave her all
so you might live.

ANCESTOR

There, claws sunk in a river snag,
hangs a wrinkly skinned

iguana as long as I am tall.
I can't explain his goiter, nor

the prickles beneath his chin.
Along his back vestigial spines

droop like a bad comb-over.
One eye he keeps on us

while we steal closer.
Why hang there in the heat,

instead of bellying up
to the mudbank?

Maybe to him, one
who must take in

whatever warmth
he's going to have,

this choking sauna's
as close to nirvana

as this incarnation's
going to get.

BLUE MORPHO

At rest, false eyes
spot us,

your legs tasting
half-fermented mango,

rippling proboscis
sipping rank juice.

One startled slash—
bright shimmer—

ocean sixty feet down,
earth seen from space,

longing held
too long

song of one long gone,
that blue.

Not what you absorb, but
what you can't take in—

that's what we see
of your beauty.

SPIRIT OF THE BAT

Hair rush, low swoop—
so those of us

stuck here on earth
know—you must be gods.

Or friends of gods,
granted chances

to push off into sky,
granted chances

to hear so well
your own voice bounced

back to you
maps the night.

Each hinge
in your wing is

an act of creation.
Each insect

you snick out of air
a witness.

You transform
obstacles

into sounds,
then dodge them.

PASSION FLOWER

Low over this narrow strand
of land between great oceans,
one named for peace,

one named for Atlas,
who lifts the sky
above the waters,

we're airborne—edging
home, returning changed
to places we know better

than to take for granted.
Over the sea
named for Caribs

nearly wiped out
by disease,
we sip iced water.

Just hours ago
we gazed into the face
of passion

flowering this morning—
pura vida
most alive

on tenuous edges
between hungry seas.
Witness this moment

set off
by our brief passage.
What came before,

what comes after,
the verge ourselves
alive, opening.

from

JUST BREATHE NORMALLY

MOVING WATER, TUCSON

Thunderclouds gathered every afternoon during the monsoons. Warm rain felt good on faces lifted to lick water from the sky. We played outside, having sense enough to go out and revel in the rain. We savored the first cool hours since summer hit.

The arroyo behind our house trickled with moving water. Kids gathered to see what it might bring. Tumbleweed, spears of ocotillo, creosote, a doll's arm, some kid's fort. Broken bottles, a red sweater. Whatever was nailed down, torn loose.

We stood on edges of sand, waiting for brown walls of water. We could hear it, massive water, not far off. The whole desert might come apart at once, might send horny toads and Gila monsters swirling, wet nightmares clawing both banks of the worst they could imagine and then some.

Under sheet lightning cracking the sky, somebody's teenaged brother decided to ride the flash flood. He stood on wood in the bottom of the ditch, straddling the puny stream. "Get out, it's coming," kids yelled. "GET OUT," we yelled. The kid bent his knees, held out his arms.

Land turned liquid that fast, water yanked our feet, stole our thongs, pulled in the edges of the arroyo, dragged whole trees root wads and all along, battering rams thrust downstream, anything you left there gone, anything you meant to go back and get, history, water so high you couldn't touch bottom, water so fast you couldn't get out of it, water so huge the earth couldn't take it, water. We couldn't step back. We had to be there, to see for ourselves. Water in a place where water's always holy. Water remaking the world.

That kid on plywood, that kid waiting for the flood. He stood and water lifted him. He stood, his eyes not seeing us. For a moment, we all wanted to be him, to be part of something so wet, so fast, so powerful, so much bigger than ourselves. That kid rode the flash flood inside us, the flash flood outside us. Artist unglued on a scrap of glued wood. For a few drenched seconds, he rode. Water took him, faster than you can believe. He kept his head up. Water you couldn't see through, water half dirt, water whirling hard. Heavy rain weighed down our clothes. We stepped closer to the crumbling shore, saw him downstream smash against the footbridge at the end of the block. Water held him there, rushing on.

"MOTHER'S FIRST WORDS AFTER THE BIRTH"

Because I was her first, no one listened when my mother cried, "It's time, it's coming!" The nurses patted her hand, crossed their legs.

"We'll tell *you*, honey, when it's getting close."

So I was almost born between floors, my mother clamping shut her thighs, some panicky orderly pinning her shoulders to the gurney. My father, a lanky teenager dreaming of a shovelhead Harley with a suicide clutch, paced.

When we were mopped up, presentable, he slouched in, reached afraid to touch my mother's flattened, baby-fine hair. His hands felt enormous, charming, full of forgiveness.

Face to the wall, my mother spoke from far away.

"I'm sorry it isn't a boy for you, honey."

Imagine being the woman who would think that, just after giving birth for the first time. Imagine her saying it out loud to her young man. Imagine her writing it down in the baby book.

THE APPLE

Mother slices the apple without sawing, twirls out the blossom end, the seeds, with one crisp swipe. Cross-sectioned womb, one for me, one for sister. Mother with one hand open and one fist clenched.

Once we took a vacation. We drove to California, went to see killer whales in too-small tanks splashing families just like ours, paddled canoes in brown water, felt our rocket shake as it took off for Tomorrowland. We stopped in Vegas on the way home. My mom forgot two pillows at the motel and insisted that we drive back for them. They were in the special pillowcases, the ones with tatting around the mouths. Dad grumbled, but he drove back.

When we got home, our friends yelled, "What'd ya do?"

"We got to sleep in a tent!" we yelled back.

Once after a car trip long enough to put us to sleep, we played possum. Both parents recognized we were pretending, limp in our dreams, just so we'd be carried into the house. Neither one slapped our legs, said, "Get up, you fakers. Walk." Instead, they scooped us up, propped us warm on their shoulders, and bumped shut the car doors gently with their hips.

Once in Tucson it snowed. Dad took home movies while Mom tried to teach us to make a snowman. We wore socks on our hands. They got wet pretty fast. Then we wanted to go inside. Our boxer dog tried to walk six inches off the ground. The last frames show Mom throwing snowballs into the arroyo. Then at the movie camera.

Once at a Musician's Union barbecue, the piñata broke just as it hit the perfect spot in its arc. Candy showered us.

Once we took to Himmel Park tomato sandwiches with Miracle Whip on Wonder Bread. No bruises on the pears. Plenty of ice in the chest. Dad pushed us on the swings. Mom tossed her hair, golden corona of soft curls backlit in the sun. They smiled at each other, smiled as if they knew something nobody else knew. Nobody that day wanted to be anywhere else. Nobody that day wanted to be anybody else. Nobody that day cried. Dad pushed us higher than we'd ever gone before, higher than the bar that held the bolts that held the chains we clutched so hard. Dad pushed us. Top of the arc—held there in midair, suspended, the chains widening, that thump scary heartbeat, then the thrill backward falling, legs bent, face down, facing the shallow graves scraped under each swing, then rising back, lifting taller even than our father reaching his huge warm gentle hand to swoop us forward, down, and amazingly up again.

MY FATHER'S WIVES #1

In lust with the whole world, my parents squirmed out of their clothes. Their teenaged bodies crashed magnificently against one another, surf undercutting the cliff where they lay. Sex was clumsy, new, unbelievable. They went at it as if they'd just invented it.

They went together like beach sand in an open eye.

They only married because I was on the way. I figured that out early. They drove to Yuma, where a new hatch of crickets writhed, a jumpy carpet, tobacco juice brown. My father's footsteps crunched and slid. Their witness, Aunt Annalise, was wearing new shoes, chunky white platform heels with eyelet cutouts showing her nylons. She didn't want to get out of the car.

"Whatd'ya think, they'll crawl up and get your wooly-booger?" Uncle Don poked at her. The four of them woke up the justice of the peace.

When the parents' screams pierced another midnight, my stomach clenched. All my fault, their misery.

NEIGHBORHOOD KIDS, TUCSON

Nelson Roush had such big buck teeth he couldn't close his lips, even to kiss. Pam Pitzer went to the Arizona State School for the Deaf and Blind, and turned our fingers into alphabets. Then our hands sang, silently. Googie Sopher was slow, we thought, until the school sent home a note saying he couldn't hear in one ear. On summer nights, we ganged up after dark, the only time cool enough to play. Murder at Midnight, Sardines, Princess and Slaves. The buds of my breasts rubbed raw on my undershirt. Johnny Mann dragged around, never wanted to do anything. He was famous for falling asleep standing up. One summer he went to visit his grandparents. When he got back, he was a regular kid, weaned off his mama's drugs. Gary Barman's dad kept their lawn perfect as a velvet carpet. Gary could fold his toes back, then walk on the tops of his feet. His arms stretched out like the Catholics' Jesus, still on the cross. We stole looks inside their church, saw Him there, roasting over hundreds of candles flickering in red glass. Linda Geiling had a swimming pool but never invited anybody over. She leapt and twirled on the dry Bermuda grass in her front yard, a dervish in July heat. She was so flexible she could do splits right leg forward, left leg forward, both legs out to the sides. She never got to watch television at home, so at our house she would sit with her nose almost on the screen. Oblivious to the world, Linda would gyrate her genitals into the rug. She ended up running away to join the Ice Capades. Really. Vicki, Robin, and Jeri Lou Watson had to go every year to the Shriners Hospital in California to get new leg braces to replace the ones they'd outgrown. Bobby Kingston found droopy, snotty balloons under the oleanders by the Catholic church. Delores Durham got $1.00 allowance *every week*. Unbelievable. She spent those dollars on single records—"Help," "Satisfaction," "Ferry Cross the Mersey," "This Diamond Ring," "Brown Eyed Girl," "Runaway." We stacked 45s on our thumbs, then slipped them as high as they would go over the big-hole spindle on her portable hi-fi. Kenny Kidwell didn't play with us any more after police found his dad in a brand-new yellow convertible, shot through the head. Self-inflicted GSW. Our first suicide. Donnie, three blocks over, was the second. He was in eighth grade and constantly practiced till he got it perfect tying a noose. Randy Fahr had bedroom eyes. He invited me swimming at his backyard pool. He tried to take off my top. When a drunk driver broke Grandpa Moen's neck, my mom sent each of us to a different neighbor so she could fly to El Cajon to be with him. I went to the Waldens' house. Kris Walden had the beautiful thick curled eyelashes models try to create with mascara. Kris and I tried walking tightrope along the footboard of her bed. I fell, straddling the wood. They couldn't stop the bleeding. Her parents took me to a strange doctor who shined a bright light between my legs, then pronounced me "intact." I curled up in the fetal position. Don McLain, Barton Lee's dad, used to trick-or-treat dressed up in camo fatigues, carrying a flask. He groveled for a shot at each house. Little kids he'd scare with his full-face ogre mask—AH-NU-NA-NU-NINI! Barton Lee was an only child. She used to say to the rest of us, "You're all figments of my imagination. I'm the only one who's real. If I forget to think of you, you'll die." We played with her anyway. She had a stack of comic books as tall as I was, a whole shelf of china dogs, a microscope.

IRON FILINGS

Down in the arroyo, we took our magnets, lifted metallic fur from black swaths in the sand. We filled film canisters, heavier than you'd believe, with whiskers of iron. The way each strand leapt onto our little red horseshoes let us know—the earth is full of attractions nobody can see.

SAND RUBIES

The best treasure came to us mostly after rain, when the arroyo rearranged itself to suit the wet. We'd have to kneel at least, or sit quietly for a long time. This meditation turned us into visionaries, ones who could see what lay buried not far beneath. Red glints, stones precious because they disappeared. Sand rubies. Deep red and transparent one moment, flecks diving out of sight the next. In this way, we learned to savor what is always there, especially when we can't see it. In this way we learned to love ephemera: the sand of the ancient ocean, this earth, this life, everything loaned for a brief time to us.

SHELTER

The big argument in the prosperous houses was this: do we build a bomb shelter or a swimming pool? (We weren't getting either one, so we didn't have this fight at home.)

During the Cuban Missile Crisis we had to take home notes. Our parents were supposed to write down who was allowed to pick us up if they couldn't get to the school. Worried, I said, "Why wouldn't you be able to come to school?" My mother snorted, then wrote on my note in her big loopy scrawl, "You shouldn't lie to little kids." She made me take that note back to school. When the principal called, the two of them had words.

Then she packed us into the Chevy and took us to see the missile silos ringing Tucson. "If a nuclear bomb hits, we'll all die together," she told us. Hardly reassuring. But I never suffered the delusion that nuclear war might create an inconvenience.

Miss Ervin was the artsy fifth grade teacher, the one who strummed her dulcimer between arithmetic and social studies while we sang "Oh Shenandoah, I love your daughter." I had no clue who Shenandoah was or what his daughter might look like, but I loved the line "A-a-way, you rolling river." I tried to picture a river wide enough to roll, a river with water in it all the time, not like the arroyos around here, dry except for a trickle or flood once a year.

Mrs. Burnham was the tough fifth grade teacher. She wasn't amused when Gary Givens connected the dots of his freckles to draw a blue ballpoint picture of Huckleberry Hound. She made him scrub his skin with rough brown paper towels and gritty pink soap that fell when we pressed up on the lever.

Above all else, Mrs. Burnham valued hard work, so mostly we worked hard. She was absolutely consistent, which I appreciated. We knew we would not get an A for an 89. But we also knew where everything was in her classroom, including each of us. When my family was coming apart, it was a comfort to know that if something bad happened to me, Mrs. Burnham would notice.

From her set jaw, we came to understand that learning was something that would benefit us later. What a shock then one day in November when she was late. She was never late. This day, though, no teacher blew her whistle on time to call us back in from the playground. The teachers came out in a hushed bunch from the multipurpose room, gathered us without speaking. Mrs. Burnham's face was rearranged. If she didn't hold it just right, it might break into a million pieces and scatter under the desks. We sat down, even the boys.

Mrs. Burnham passed out construction paper, the big sheets. She told us, "We're going to take the rest of the afternoon to think, boys and girls. Let's think about what our country means to us. Let's think about—" Then a color I'd never seen took over her face. She went to her desk, fumbled for the chair, and put her face on the blotter. Her back, her shoulders, jerked. The more she tried not to, the harder she cried. When she could lift her face, she looked out at us. She looked far, as if we were in the foreground and she wanted to survey the whole land. I knew right then that our world had changed, but how?

"I have something to tell you," she said, swallowing. "President Kennedy has been shot."

Kids looked around as much as they could without moving. We looked around as if we were in trouble, blamed.

After school, boys ran to the arroyo, then shot each other with mesquite sticks. Those idiots took a ridiculously long time to die.

At home, Mom crunched aluminum foil onto each of the rabbit ears. Even Walter Cronkite looked shaky. Over and over a convertible rolled down a street. Then guys riding the bumper jumped into the backseat. Over and over, the pictures of Jackie, her clothes all bloodied.

I imagined the doctors up to their elbows trying to put the president's head back together. We all hoped. We hoped the way you hope Romeo and Juliet won't really die, even though Shakespeare tells you from the get-go they will.

I imagined everything leaking out, everything he had learned, everything he dreamed, all his secrets.

Hours paced around. Walter Cronkite's voice: "President Kennedy is dead."

For the next four days, nobody went to school, nobody went to work, nobody left the grainy Philco. We watched a parade, immaculate horses, then one horse with no rider, the boots backward in the stirrups. A little boy saluted, little boy in short pants. Wasn't he cold? Why didn't anybody snuggle him? And his sister, on display, in shock. No hugs. Their mother was scary, draped in black, her grief. That veil, nearly sheer, no privacy.

Life Magazine showed up every week. My dad said that was one reason he quit the safe job his dad got him as a letter carrier. He just couldn't bear every blasted week to be weighed down by *Life*.

On the back cover, an advertiser's idea of a doctor wore on his forehead a round disk about as big as the lid of a Mason jar. It had a hole in the middle. I never did find out what that was for. No doctor I ever saw had one. This doctor leaned forward so you would trust him, or if you didn't trust him, you would at least obey. People obeyed doctors in those days. You were supposed to hear the caption in his voice, the voice of Richard Chamberlain in *Dr. Kildare*: "I recommend Camels for all my patients who smoke."

Dogs and fire hoses, one week. German Shepherds and open nozzles set on little kids, kids dressed up in Sunday School clothes. I was terrified that people would do such a thing. Maybe we'd be next. I knew where the closest hydrant was. I asked my mother why grown men would hurt kids like this.

"Because they're afraid," she said.

"What country is this?" I asked.

"Every country in the world," she said.

"But right now, which country is doing this right now?"

"Ours. Right now it's our country."

HOMECOMING

The year my uncle Jack came back from Vietnam I remember as unbearably hot. We swiped chunks of two-by-fours heaped by cracking slabs poured for houses exactly like ours and set the wood on melting asphalt so our kickstands would hold. Otherwise, they sank in, left pedals digging their own graves.

The developer shaved off all the desert plants and planted tract homes. We still found a few survivors—horny toads in shady corners, kangaroo rats in the dog chow.

We made a banner—Welcome Home Jack—and draped it across the garage door at my uncle Dan's house. The first night Jack got in, we grilled steaks from American Meat Company and made a big salad. (I peeled the cucumbers, careful to rub the cut end in a circle three times to draw out the bitterness.)

When I first saw Jack, I held back. His eyes let me know that a hug was all right, welcome even. He looked skinny, tired, maybe sick. Mom had warned us not to ask about the war, not to congratulate him on his medals, not to mention his wife and child. Fay, his rich, spoiled teenaged British bride, had languished in Mountain Home, Idaho, where she gave birth, then grown bored in Sausalito where they had set up house. She packed up their infant son and returned to her father's mansion across the ocean.

All I knew was that Jack was a hero. He flew small spotter planes close to the ground and dropped smoke for the bombers to use as targets. Only years later would I begin to comprehend how that meant he could see the people there, no way to tell who was an enemy, could see the starved kids, the animals, could see whole villages of huts that would be destroyed. He could also see US troops he might not be able to shield or help. He had to see what was left of many of his friends or to imagine what was never seen again. He had to see shapes zipped into body bags.

The second night, a hot night, my mom put on a pot of her famous Swiss steak. She scrubbed and poked the baked potatoes. Fresh sun tea for the kids, beer for the adults. She worked all day to get the house ready. My dad took off on a motorcycle ride just before Jack arrived. I was glad Mom and Jack had those few hours together, glad they had a private moment.

But Dad didn't come back. The table was set. We had finally just poured the tea over the ice when my dad roared up, scraping the Harley's back wheel over the straggling African daisies my mom kept shaded. He loves me, he loves me not.

"Jack!" he yelled, "Come look at my bike!" Jack went to check out the '64 Sportster, cherried, candy-apple red with black trim. Dad was laughing, loud, his bar laugh. Jack told Dad dinner was on the table. Then he ducked back inside.

Dad drew in big lungs full of beer breath. He drew open the sliding glass door and yelled, "Hey, honey, let's not go to any trouble. Let's go out for dinner and drinks."

He went over to the splay-legged couch where Jack was sitting, his back not touching the Naugahyde. Dad never even asked how Jack was. Instead, he started talking motorcycles. "We have a dirt track out in the desert, want to come see?"

"Not right now." Jack could hardly look at him. I felt so sorry that Jack, just home from the war, had to see this.

Mom had that eerie calm that meant her temper was plumping up her whole body. She calmly walked into the kitchen, put on hot mitts and dumped the whole pot, sauce and steak, in the trash. Then she unjammed the junk drawer and dug around for our split-handled ball-peen hammer.

Whoosh of cool air released as she scraped open the sliding door. She walked, deadly calm, over to my father's motorcycle. Like a musician, she held the hammer head high, waited for the right breath.

Then she exhaled. On cue, she sank the rounded end with cool precision *tank tank tank* across the sexy paint until we could have set up Chinese checkers.

My father ran out, stared. Stared. Then he grabbed her wrists, hard enough to bruise. He grabbed her wrists and tried to force her back into the house. Jack came to the door and said, "Don't. You. Hit. Her. Don't." My mom splayed herself like a big X across the opening. They struggled, the grownups.

I'm fifteen. My usual routine: crawl out of bed at 4:30, finish homework while it's quiet, throw in a load of wash, wake up the kids. Shower, brush teeth, throw on a Madras shift, tug a brush through my waist-length hair. Worry that it's too wavy (not stylish). Wake the kids again. Help them with cereal and milk, if we have any. Cut them a hunk of welfare commodity cheese if we don't. Get them washed and dressed and out the door. Run to Palo Verde, just in time for 7:00 a.m. Office Skills, where we clatter along on manual typewriters and push ourselves toward 100 words a minute in shorthand.

I'd put in a full day at school, then run home, hoping the little kids made it back all right, that the Siefarth twins didn't ambush them, that nobody's knees were bloody.

One morning, though, I stumbled out into the predawn living room and cracked my shin. What the—? I snapped on the hall light, saw the rollaway bed set up crossways. There in their full glory were my mom and some guy, spooned, passed out. Naked. Mom's face was smeared, her breasts sucked purple.

The whole place smelled rank. Spilled beer, full ashtrays, sour flesh, scorched carpet.

She worked two dead-end jobs, collating multiple listings all day and waiting tables at a dive, the Rio Rita, all night. She'd bring home the best of a bad lot and sway to country music—"Make the world go away . . ." They'd guzzle cheap booze, smoke cheap cigarettes, smash themselves against one another.

Most nights, though, she had the sense to take them back into her room, to shut the door. I had to figure out how to make them disappear, how to make sure the kids didn't have to see this. I ran cold water over a washrag, patted it against her face.

"Mom? MOM?"

She shoved the cloth away. "What the—?"

"It's morning. The kids will be up any minute."

"Shit." She tried turning over.

"No, you have to get up, right now."

"Says who?"

"Please." By then I was furious, crying. I couldn't help it. What did she think she was doing? Why didn't she even try to watch out for us?

I didn't know who this loser was, couldn't even guess how he was going to hurt her. Or maybe he was just a two-hundred-pound balsa wood airplane, a flimsy toy she'd fly once and then crash, splintering.

"Shake me again, you're on restriction," she slurred.

Like you're ever around to enforce it, I thought. My mind flashed to the test today, midterm in geometry, tried to remember how to use what's given to do proofs.

"Now. Get up." My voice was the voice I used on kids, firm. She roused, asked for her glasses, listed down the hallway, her breasts swaying.

That left me with the guy. I wanted to stab him, burn him, make him pay. His pimpled butt. I pulled the sheet to his shoulder, then poured a glass of ice water on his neck. He bolted up, yelling. Then he saw me, and tried to figure out where he was. I could see him backpedaling, trying to return to a place where everything in this picture made sense.

"You need to go home now," I said.

"Okay," he mumbled.

"Now," I insisted.

He felt around for his jockey shorts, and I went into the kitchen. He dressed fast, I'd give him that much, and shut the front door as quietly as he could.

I was just reaching to get down the Cheerios when my little brother padded up behind me. I jumped.

"Hey, you scared me," I smiled.

"Who was that man?" John asked sadly.

"What man?"

"I got up to go to the bathroom. I saw them." And then he was crying. I held him and held him. "Why is this happening?" he asked.

"I don't know, honey. I just don't know."

LIPS, TUCSON, 1969

My mother had a luscious mouth, sumptuous. A venomous neighbor, angry about something else, sneered, "You have nigger lips." My mother looked her directly in the eyes: "Why, thank you!" she said gently. The neighbor, disarmed, didn't know what to do.

Just because Sue couldn't stand spit, my mother gathered slobber between her big lips and slathered Sue's thrashing face. "Good night!"

In her coffin, my mother's lips looked like wax, Halloween lips without red dye #2. Someone had brushed on a dry orange color, outlining a prim little mouth inside the edges of her lips.

Wires held open her nostrils. Her lips were stitched shut, not very neatly. The undertaker's hairdresser couldn't do much with my mom's thin hair, hair she called WW hair, World's Worst. Each fine strand lay flat against her skull. Her hands, crossed over her chest, posed like carved suet.

Why did they put the family behind a curtain, like the zonk prize on *Let's Make a Deal?* After everyone else had filed out, the man with the black suit and funny smell motioned that we should walk down a little hallway that led back to the mortuary chapel.

It was there, yawning open, the ridiculous box. We paid way too much, money we didn't have, though water and worms would eat through fancy wood just as easily as plain. My uncle, guilty, had refused my mom a $500 loan. She was drinking heavily, and he was probably right not to bail her out again. So he almost went for the concrete-lined vault. I had to say out loud, "We don't need that." The man with the funny smell fixed me with a look.

And there it was, her body. It held me once, then pushed me sixteen years ago out into this world. It hit my sister Ginny every day, and the rest of us when we didn't get out of the way. It cradled each of us, as if we were miracles. It was sexed and sexed and very little loved by men. It was a constant source of confusion for those of us who loved the woman it held. We never knew if that body would be on our side or if it was another threat, disguised as Mom.

After the divorce, things slid downhill fast. Our whole household was an arroyo collapsing in on itself. Dad married Crazy Marcia, a bottle blonde with a serious affection for prescription painkillers. We nicknamed her daughters for their passions: the Nympho, the Pyro, the Klepto.

Eating an orange at Marcia's house was a project. First, we'd post a sentry. Then one kid would lift an orange from the bowl on the table. That kid would walk fast into the bathroom. Everybody who wanted in on it came into the bathroom too. We'd peel the fruit, divide the sections exactly evenly (you cut and I choose), then swallow the fruit almost without chewing. We washed our hands and faces, brushed our teeth. We flushed the orange peels, wiped the counter.

When Marcia came out of her room in the late afternoon, she'd know right away that something had changed. She'd count and count the oranges. "Eight. There should be eight."

"Seven," we'd say. "This time you bought lucky seven, remember?"

The day of the moonwalk I had a date. Chuck Quimby came early to pick me up. We couldn't leave the house, though, because Marcia had an episode. She had plucked out every hair in both eyebrows, and held a stencil high across her forehead to pencil in new ones. She couldn't get them right. Couldn't. Her hands wouldn't cooperate. Irritation slid into hysteria, and Marcia got clingy. I pictured techniques they taught in Junior Lifesaving, the ways to keep a panicked swimmer from drowning you too.

We erased the jagged arches over her perplexed eyes. We fed her crushed ice. Her face, bald and sallow, sank in on itself. She looked powdery, like the surface of the moon, marked by boots, by men.

Finally, she slept.

"One small step for man . . ."

LOCKET

One of the few objects handed down to me when my mother died is a small rectangular locket engraved with a spray of wildflowers. Might be gold, might be plate, I don't care. It was hers. In her high school graduation portrait, it rests in the hollow between her new breasts, nestled in folds of angora. Inside, a miniature photo of her, very young, her smile wide as the Milky Way. On the other side, all sleek muscles and slicked back Wildroot hair, grins a boy, a young man barely, cocky and sure he's good looking so why not cut his eyes at the camera, why not lean back on two legs of his chair, the sun's out, he's got gas money and a pretty girl, surf's up, man.

During the long fifteen years of their marriage, my parents yelled at each other, didn't even agree on a topic, just yelled in general. I took solace in the knowledge of that young man, imagined he was my real dad, lost to war or adventure, his presence there next to her heart a repudiation, male and sexy, of every reproach my father could throw at her. The self she carried in that locket grinned, eternally joyous, sassy as a skirt of giant kelp, stinging bare midriff and thighs, salty as her first good kiss, not shared with my father. Nobody recalls that boy's name now, not my grandmother, not my mother's high school friends, not Uncle Harry.

And my father, what did he carry, man with no amulet to protect him, and the heavy freight of his Nazarene father always on his shoulders. Pressed down on his knees in surrender to a God he never really met, my father shook off his father's zealous palm and knelt between the knees of any willing female. "Never pass up a chance at pussy," he told Harry, who knew even at thirteen there was something basic wrong with that advice. He wasn't sure what though because all the other guys were laughing and nodding, blowing smoke rings and French inhaling. He was the youngest one there and counted himself lucky to be allowed to tag along. So Harry swallowed hard, he told me, swallowed the hard knot in his throat and made himself think about motorcycles, baseball, ham, pistachios, anything but how his sister's, my mother's, face would look when she found out who she'd married.

HOLY MAN, 1992

Once, on the island of Kauai, a woman took me to a Buddhist ceremony. We stopped first at some cabins left from the time sugar cane was a major crop. We gave a ride to two women who lived in the fields.

In a modest house, we gathered. The brass bowl sang. The altar held rice, oranges, a handmade scroll. After chants and meditation, the holy man who had traveled far to be there asked people what was in their hearts. A few people spoke, and he spoke back, calm, patient. He talked about spiritual vibrations loose in the world, as real as radio signals. We cannot hear them until we tune in. But they're there, as surely as air.

I trusted him.

I asked how I could help her, my mother who didn't want to be here.

He bowed his head, waited. Then he said quietly, "A child can atone for her mother's death wish."

He did not say how. I did not ask.

It was a great gift, this possibility.

My mother had been twenty years in the ground. No matter.

At my best moments, I tune in.

TURQUOISE DRESS

Just before I started fourth grade, my mom brought home from a rummage sale a little turquoise dress with puffed sleeves. The fabric, sheer as running water, cascaded over my head and baptized my body. So cool. Like wearing my own personal cloud, in a place where rain's a rare blessing. A black velvet ribbon tied around the waist. Not in back like the sashes on little-girl dresses, but in front, a touch of elegance I tied myself. I slid the bow over my left hip.

That year, my teacher Mrs. Garner opened the world of the arts to me, took time away from teaching us the exports of Brazil to have us choreograph our own dances, write and act out our own plays, put down on paper our private songs and stories.

She had as much fun as we did building the Amazon out of chicken wire and papier-mâché. I spent the most time on our life-size crocodile, mixing just the right shades to paint the ivory teeth and jungle-green toenails. When he wasn't there after Christmas vacation, I was sure he had whipped his tail and torpedoed away underwater.

I wore the turquoise dress every day I could get away with it. It was the first garment I learned how to wash out by hand. Hung on a painted wire hanger (I was careful to choose one that wouldn't rust), the dress dried quick as a good laugh.

In the turquoise dress, anything could happen. I could fly to school, arriving for patrol duty before my feet even knew where we were going. I could play my stop sign like a guitar, and sing "Cielito Lindo" to the Catalina Mountains. Loitering at recess by the ramada, I would *look* ordinary, but I could be swimming with manta rays and sharks. Watching the world through my sleeve of water, I could hold my breath as long as I wanted and live for years under the sea.

Powerful, I could walk home with Karen Pfantz, even though the other girls would make fun of us. Karen wore faded old lady dresses from the bargain bin at the disabled vets store. Karen got the lowest grade, always. After every test, she lifted the lid of her desk and let big drops water her notebooks. The popular girls jeered, "You don't like *Karen,* do you?"

"Just ignore them," I told her. She tried. Her horsey face gathered itself up as if she were trying to refuse the bit. We took the long way to her house, playing under the footbridges where they crossed the arroyos, getting a drink out of the Roush's hose. We wondered out loud if their lives were better in the Roush's house since Mrs. Roush painted the top half lavender. She left the bottom half bare adobe.

Eventually, though, we had to take Karen home. Her father would rouse himself out of the stupor of that day and growl. I stayed as long as I could, knowing that as long as I was there he wouldn't do to Karen what he did to her every day after school. That turquoise dress made me brave so I could stay. Then I'd go home to see if Mom was drunk or sober.

One day, Karen didn't come to school. Nobody said anything. When I asked, the nurse told me she moved to Florida.

Blessings on you, Karen Pfantz, wherever you are, I thought.

A dust devil swept the playground, and I crouched down so my turquoise dress could shield my bare legs. Red—all I could see with my eyes hidden in the crook of my elbow was red, the waxy tulip shade seen through closed lids. As I stood up after the storm, a stampede of boys headed my way from the tetherball courts. *Ya-Ya, Ya-Ya,* they bellowed. One grabbed my sleeve, hard.

Almost slow motion, how the fabric gave way. Almost an early-morning dream, when you don't know if you're asleep or awake. The sleeve's seam held. Threads all across the back let go quietly, no great rip. Karen, never complaining. My dress hung down over my bare shoulder, my slip strap in plain sight.

Where did they come from, those big gulping sobs? I hardly ever cried, and never in front of people. Even when the bell rang, I couldn't stop. The boy, defending himself before the playground monitor, said, "Why are you so upset? It was an old dress. You wear it every day."

The playground monitor meant to console. "He only does that because he likes you, you know."

I shuffled in, huddled under my desk lid. My cloud had torn. I couldn't mend it.

Mrs. Garner took me aside, murmured, "You don't need a special dress to be powerful. It was just a reminder."

Do we take scars as evidence of injury, or as evidence of healing? Do we bear scars of one life? What about scars handed down, scars we pass along?

WHAT COMES NEXT

What comes next, I learn from Joe, again and again.

Around the blind curve comes a kid, screaming illegally down the bike path on his four-wheel ATV. Joe sees him, thinks, "Oh, man, this is gonna hurt." The ATV's suspension catches Joe's front tire, crushing it rim to hub, twisting. Joe flies over his handlebars, over the kid and the four-wheeler, and lands on his knees on the path. "Wasn't so bad," Joe thinks.

He jumps up, cursing the dumb son of a bitch, and runs to where I am lying. I'm curled on my side, back to the concrete. Both sides of my helmet are gouged and scraped. My right knee bleeds around imbedded gravel. A little trickle of blood leaks from my lips. Joe tries to get some response, but I am out.

Witnesses stop right away and call 911. A man leaps the fence and holds my head.

The ambulance can't drive all the way to where we are, so it eases out across the gravel. Then paramedics have to hoof it. Two people hold my head still as they strap me to a backboard.

I open one eye but the sun's too bright.

While he talks to police, Joe watches paramedics tending me, then sees that they're heading for the ambulance. He tries to run, to keep up, and feels his back seize.

I'm under a door covered with sandbags. Muddy water's rising. My hips sink deeper into muck. I can't open my eyes until I know what's in this water. The weight crushing my chest grows heavier. Am I wearing armor? My lungs fill with wet concrete.

The nurses, attentive, calm, brave, admit they were scared too. Some I was too groggy to remember, but I remember the kind one who was hugely pregnant, how I felt guilty each time I made her walk on her swollen ankles. And the quick slender one with glasses who stayed with me when panic lurched into my throat. And the ones who cleaned me, cleaned up after me, the ones who wiped my body when I could not. At first, I was embarrassed, deeply. Then I watched them, watched carefully the dignity of their work wiping away the indignities of injury.

"What happened to us?"

I watch Joe draw in a deep breath. I know then I've asked and asked many times. And he has answered. He gathers himself, trying hard. What could he say that would stay heard?

BEFORE THE TUBE

Before the tube choked off words, I spoke. To my husband I said what might be the last. I barely understood what they intended, only that they wanted desperately to help. After the first numbing, I fought. After the second, my resisting, instinctive, was no match for their gentleness. For forty-five minutes an aide squeezed plastic bulb-fuls of air into my lungs. Weeks later, reading dictated notes, I find out a machine breathed for me for two days.

Where are they, those days? Where are those days that slip away as surely as breath?

Ever notice that when you get that advice, "Just breathe normally," you can never do it?

When you're handed a six-foot rosy boa, when a tarantula tangles his arm's hair in yours, when you sneak up with a Dixie cup to catch a scorpion, when you're maintaining in front of your friend's parents, when before surgery you're counting backward from one hundred, when for the first time you fit a snorkel between your teeth and put your mask into water, when the dog they said doesn't bite clearly intends to, when you tell that necessary lie, when your scuba instructor tells you to take the giant stride into two hundred feet of ocean, when they slide you tight into the MRI tube, when you stand to give your speech, when yellow cups of oxygen fall from the plane's ceiling, when the respiratory therapist clips together your nostrils, when the dentist packs your mouth with cotton logs, when you get the news you've been waiting for, when you get the news you've been dreading, when you stand up before god and everybody to pledge your love to your mate, just breathe normally.

Next door to me in intensive care, they bring in a young woman who has survived a head-on crash that killed six other people. She's completely cut loose from this earth—doesn't know who or where she is, doesn't know what year it is. The nurse keeps reminding her that her mother's on the way. But the mom's coming up from Utah, so the daughter's in limbo for now. She cannot identify the parts of her own body. They've told her that she's eighteen. They've not yet told her she's a widow.

I cannot see. I cannot see her, but I can hear.

WILDERNESS

The voice yelling in the wilderness doesn't know what year it is, doesn't know how old it is, doesn't know its own name.

The voice pleading in the wilderness can't recall how it got here, doesn't know where this is, can't locate its hands.

The voice echoing in the wilderness can't guess how many fingers or why. No matter how intensive the care, doesn't know it's married to silence.

SHOWER

When you have traveled to the edge, looked over, pulled back, when a machine has drawn breath for you for a day, for two, when your bruises, travel stickers for trips you don't remember, haven't faded, but you've come back, back to some sense of self, what do you want?

First, a shower. You cannot believe the stench near death, how it clings. But you have to get a special dispensation, and help. The doc says all right, just not too hot. It's slow, leaning down the hallway on Joe, the IV stand tangling. The shower has thank god a chair, but no hand-held head. Superhuman strength this will take. No. Just more than you've got.

Aiming the body toward water, you take no breath for granted. Aiming toward water the body. Aiming toward cleansing, toward breath.

DR. MARTINO

Dr. Martino, the neurologist, asks me to perform a few small tasks. First he tells me three things to remember—sailboat, button, shoe. Then he asks me to walk heel to toe across his office. I'm bad at this, and list far enough to one side that I have to grab twice at the exam table. He checks my reflexes. I catch the little rubber hatchet before it thunks the broken places on my right knee. Looking deep into my eyes, he tells me what he knows about the third cranial nerve. Hard to predict if and when it might mend. He asks me not to look at what he places in my hand. Wild leaps, electrical, chemical, from fingertips to brain to lips. I say, "Penny. Paper clip. Key. Rubber band."

What could be more simple? Until the day we cannot do this. What then do we hold in our hand?

The least injured part of me wants to look him straight in the soul, this doctor of missed connections, and say correctly, "Shooting star. Red aurora. Mist forest. Life after this. Life."

He describes how the body rewires itself after insults to the brain. Most of my infarcts occur across the back of the brain, along the base of the skull, home to balance and memory. The one dead spot at the front of the brain may affect decisions, judgment. I glance at Joe, at my nieces, and know by their almost grins that I'm in trouble. "It's that judgment thing . . ."

Dr. Martino asks me to remember those objects he mentioned at the beginning of the exam. I think. I picture my Great-Grandma Langley's buttonhook, and recall button, shoe. And just as the sun sets, drifting out on a twilit Fijian lagoon, that sailboat.

Great mysteries, how we take in, sort through, retrieve, release each moment millions of bits of stimuli. How each of us hoards a ragtag collection that makes us exactly us, no one else.

ALTARS

On Día de los Muertos, people set up altars to welcome back those who have gone before. In the Sonoran Desert, where the dead are said to cherish fragrances, paths of marigolds help the ancestors find their way.

It's not mournful at all. Music, singing, dancing, a candle-light vigil. Huge spreads of food. After the dead have tasted their favorite dishes, living people feast on homemade tortillas hot off the *comal*. Husky tamales—meat, green corn, sweet. Skull-shaped candies, breads, cookies. The gritty bonedust of *panocha*.

Saladitos turn every mouth into a watering hole. Fry bread starts out flat, then puffs in hot oil, its emptiness honeyed.

~

On the altars, pictures of loved ones out of reach. Loved ones forever the age they were when they left. Tokens of lives. A fishing lure. Skate key. Spurs. Carved *bate* for frothing hot chocolate. Pierced earrings. Locket. Dancing shoes, size tiny. A lizard-skin cowboy boot, planted with jumping cactus.

Calacas—skeletons riding motorcycles, getting married, having babies. Skeletons at typewriters, skeletons on the rollercoaster. Skeletons playing billiards, every ball on the table a skull. Calacas riding horseback, their holsters flapping. Calacas playing cello and violin, the tune just beyond our hearing.

~

DÍA DE LOS MUERTOS, WHIDBEY ISLAND

To celebrate that we are not among them, we choose Day of the Dead for our first post-wreck ride. We air up the tires, strap on our helmets, take deep breaths. Balance is still tricky. I can't quite tell what's flat and what's not, can't quite tell when my foot will touch ground. Extra dark sunglasses give my eye a break—when one pupil doesn't react, sunshine hurts.

I force out of my mind visions of falling, visions of me and the bike tangled in blackberry brambles, visions of cars swerving but not missing. Every muscle in my body is on alert. It's as if I have to give orders for each motion.

The focus this morning reminds me of the day I got glasses, after a childhood of seeing blurry. Each blade of grass stands out, distinct. Each chip of gravel, each glint of glass. To mount, I lean my bike so far over the pedal touches. Joe holds me steady while I balance on one foot. My right leg, the hurt leg, clears the hurdle, fishes a moment in midair, finds the pedal. I straighten, balance, breathe.

I look both ways, outside, inside. We push off, wobbly, into the rest of our lives.

NOTES

New Poems

The poems in *Placing Our Feet with Care on This Earth* honor Eloise Klein Healy and Colleen Rooney. Among many other talents, Colleen is a naturalist and a student of the human brain. Eloise, marvelous friend and poet, has a new and selected volume entitled *A Wild Surmise.*

"Geology of Wonder"

The young writer asking us to list our fears is Sherry Simpson. Judith Kitchen and Stan Rubin make cameo appearances. Eva Saulitis's book *Becoming Earth* illuminates the time I mention here.

"Green Up"

Craquelure—the pattern of fine cracks in varnish or paint on the surface of a work of art

Impossible Grace

The poems in *Impossible Grace* honor Eva Saulitis, marine biologist, poet, essayist, oboist, gardener. Her whole life Eva looked for ways to make meaning, via art, music, meditation, friendships, science, and writing.

"Touching What's Wild"

kapu—taboo, forbidden
kiawe—mesquite
lilikoi—Hawaiian passionfruit

"The Pie Dance"

Vog—forms when volcanic spume mixes with clouds over the Big Island

Esperanza's Hair

"Landlady"

la boda bellísima—the most beautiful wedding
con mariachis, un baile, y mucha comida—with musicians, a dance, and a lot of food
mi hijita—a term of affection, my little daughter

"Pancho Villa Meets El Mudo, the Deaf Shopkeeper"

Thank you to Angela Watson, who let me borrow this story from her life.

el mudo—the mute one
frijoles indios—wild food, Indian beans

"Welldigger"
fyrstikker—wooden match

The Circle of Totems

"Glass Rattlesnakes and the Three Incomparable Daughters of Marisol"
Alegría—happiness
Tristeza—sadness
Deseo—desire

"First Thing in the Morning, Éclairs, Lightning"
socorro—help

"Cinco de Mayo"
por qué—why
ese, vato—bro, dude
Xicanindio—band's name, combining Chicano and Indian
las hijas—literally, the daughters; in slang, good-looking girls
los viejitos—old folks
las cumbias—popular dances, originally from Colombia
aquí—here
el borracho—the drunk

"The Circle of Totems"
In this poem the devilfish the boy hunts is a cold-water octopus.

When I first stepped foot in Alaska, I looked up at the totem poles at Saxman and realized that the world has much more to teach me. "The Circle of Totems" is not "the story" of that powerful place, nor "the story" of one particular pole. Instead, it is an offering of what happened in the imagination of a newcomer, a woman curious about the inside story, the story nobody can know for sure. How would that boy feel, knowing that the tide was rising, knowing he couldn't pull free? Imagining the life of another person—perhaps compassion might begin this way.

Tlingit oral traditions and the carvings themselves offer the depth of thousands of years of knowing this place. I respectfully offer the perspective of a stranger in awe of the natural beauty and the incredible art that exists there. I honor the parallel nature of our lives.

Wings Moist from the Other World

"Young Boy Dancing at Playa los Muertos"

timbales—shallow, single-headed metal drums

guitarrón—oversized Mexican bass guitar

mariachis—musicians

Norteño—a style of corrido music from northern Mexico

merengue—a dance style originating in the Dominican Republic that's now popular throughout Latin America and the American Southwest

kikiriki-ki—what roosters say in Spanish

"The Provider"

George Wallace was the governor of Alabama during the civil rights movement. At his inauguration he proclaimed, "Segregation now, segregation tomorrow, segregation forever." He stood at the entrance to the University of Alabama and attempted to prevent black students from enrolling. (Much later in life he disavowed segregation.)

"Rapt"

Along the Haines Highway in Alaska, there's a five-mile section of the Chilkat River that remains open after other rivers have frozen. Eagles gather there by the hundreds to feed at the Chilkat Bald Eagle Preserve.

"Short History of One Hour's Desire"

charango—a small Andean stringed instrument traditionally made from the shell of anarmadillo

cuíca—sexy Brazilian friction drum with a wide range in pitch

Underground Rivers

"Too Soon after Rain"

sopa fideo—hearty Mexican soup thickened with vermicelli

"Easter, Grave Tending"

hardanger—traditional white-on-white Norwegian openwork embroidery

"Hillclimb"

Greeves and Ducati are brands of motorcycles.

"Ajo Lily"

ajo—garlic

jojoba—a plant from the Sonoran Desert; its oil has many uses

"The Story of Light"

babiche—rawhide strips for binding snowshoes

issum—seal pup

"Bear Plan, Brooks Range"

Arrigetch—the Arrigetch Peaks are rugged spires of granite in the Endicott section of the Brooks Range in northern Alaska, now part of Gates of the Arctic National Park.

Blaze

"Elegy for Getz"

This poem honors the jazz and bossa nova saxophonist Stan Getz. The rhythms of this poem come from Antônio Carlos Jobim's song "Águas de Março" ("Waters of March").

bossa—bossa nova, a form of Brazilian music and dance

favelas—slums

cachaça—potent Brazilian liquor distilled from sugar cane juice

"Wide Icy River"

On windy mountain passes in Alaska, tall poles with bent orange tips mark the edges of the road. During whiteouts, sometimes you lose sight of one before you can see the next.

Gnawed Bones

"Albóndigas"

albóndigas—meatball soup with rice

cominos—cumin

ajo—garlic

cilantro—Mexican herb

cebolla—onion

caldo—broth

"Land Fraud Nosebleed"

caliche—rock-hard, light-colored layer of soil cemented together by lime

Apache tears—childhood term for obsidian

"Go to the Broom Closet and Pick Out a Stick"

These are square dance calls:

Allemande left with your left hand.
Ladies Center Back to the Bar.
Hinge and Flutter. Flare the Star.
Swing your partner, right and left grand.

Toucan Nest

"Genesis, Quetzal"

vest of drip tips—In the rainforests of Costa Rica where the quetzal lives, many plants have adapted to shed water. Their leaves are waxy or glossy and come to a point. On the quetzal's body, the plumage on each side resembles the points of drip tips.

"Blue-Gray Tanager, Here, Gone"

pájaro—bird

"Keeping Loud Ones Quiet"

los loros—the parrots

"Sloth"

perezosa—sloth

"Venom"

víbora—snake
hermosa—beautiful
peligrosa—dangerous

"Getting Away"

páramo—a high moor not good for farming; a divide
Pedro Páramo—the earthshattering novel by Juan Rulfo, the grandfather of the Latin American "boom" in literature in the sixties and seventies
Talamancas—mountain range in Costa Rica; some parts rise from sea level to twelve thousand feet
cuneiform—an ancient system of writing using a stylus to mark clay tablets
fuerte—strong

"Painted Cart with No Oxen"

cajón—the box, the back part of a cart

"Burnt Fields"

víboras—snakes
zapatos—shoes
café con leche—coffee with milk
guaro—alcoholic drink distilled from sugar cane
el baile en Sábado—Saturday night dance

"Passion Flower"

pura vida—pure life, a lively greeting and a farewell in Costa Rica

Just Breathe Normally

"Moving Water, Tucson"

arroyo—desert riverbed, usually dry (until a flash flood surges through)

ocotillo—tall desert plant that looks like thorny dead sticks most of the year

horny toad—genus *Phrynosoma*, horned lizard

Gila monster—venomous lizard of the Sonoran Desert

"Altars"

comal—large cast iron griddle

panocha—coarse sugary candy

saladitos—Mexican dried salted plums

bate—or molinillo, a carved turned-wood beater for frothing hot chocolate

calacas—skeletons, also the figures of skeletons created for Day of the Dead

ACKNOWLEDGMENTS

New Poems

Cutthroat, A Journal of the Arts, Truth to Power issue: "Parenthood, Unplanned"; *Soundings*, Summer 2017: "Parenthood, Unplanned"; *Cirque*, December 2011: "Stop Bath"; Poetry video, "Stop Bath," 2014, www.youtube.com/watch?v=SWph2bXOSiY; *Bosque*, 2013: "Shape-shifters," "The Poems You Cannot Write Right Now," "Placing Our Feet with Care on This Earth," "The Basics"; *North Chicago Review*, 2013: "How to Live," "Anyone Who Comes Here Must Be Transformed"; *Sparks: A Conversation in Poems and Paintings*, a collaboration with painter Kesler Woodward, exhibit opened September 11, 2015, at the Alaska Humanities Forum, Anchorage, Alaska; *Alaska Quarterly Review*, Spring & Summer 2016 issue, and online: *Sparks: A Conversation in Poems and Paintings* with paintings, poems, and a transcript of a conversation with Kesler Woodward: "The Conversation," "Three Blues," "Geology of Wonder," "Sun at the Horizon," "Green Up," "Listening among Birches," "Letter to One Who's Gone Before," "Succession," "Sideways Walking," "Kiss," "Lilt, Patter, Bound"; *Cutthroat, A Journal of the Arts*, 2016: "Becoming Earth," "Touching What's Wild," "Valentine for Eva," "Choices," "Strong Enough"; *Cascadia Review*, May 2016: "Reading Out Loud the Whole Book," "Lists," "Holy, the Soup," "Eva's Cairn," "The Holiness of the Ground."

from **Esperanza's Hair**

University of Alabama Press, 1985

AGNI Review: "The Apple"; AWP Anniversary Awards: "Esperanza's Hair"; *Graduate English Papers*: "A Crack in the Balanced Ship"; *Laundromat*: "Landlady," "A Crack in the Balanced Ship"; *The Louisville Review*: "Welldigger," "The Lever between Her Breasts"; the *Missouri Review*: "Esperanza's Hair"; *New Mexico Humanities Review*: "Pancho Villa Meets El Mudo, the Deaf Shopkeeper"; *Poets On: Regrets*: "Jigsaw Puzzles"; *Writers' Forum*: "Landlady."

from **The Circle of Totems**

University of Pittsburgh Press, 1988

Black Warrior Review: "The Circle of Totems"; *Colorado Review*: "Owl/Beating"; *5 AM*: "Cinco de Mayo"; *Hayden's Ferry Review*: "The Waitress's Kid"; *Heartland*: "The Circle of Totems"; *Permafrost*: "Blue Apples"; *Prairie Schooner*: "First Thing in the Morning, Éclairs, Lightning."

from **Wings Moist from the Other World**

University of Pittsburgh Press, 1994

Alaska Quarterly Review: "White Figurehead at Isla Negra," "Hanna Zoe," "Glacier, Calving," "Exit Glacier"; *American Poetry Review*: "The Run of Silvers," "Short History of One Hour's

Desire," "Three Notes from a Wooden Flute"; *Cream City Review*: "Rapt"; *CutBank*: "Why Ira Pratt Cocked His Head Like That"; *Hayden's Ferry Review*: "Hunting Scorpions"; *Iowa Woman*: "Creamer's Field," "Graveyard Shift, 22nd & Tucson Boulevard"; *The James River Review*: "Melt"; *MĀNOA*: "Ira Pratt's Charts of the Stars", "The Provider"; *New Virginia Review*: "Clitoris"; *Permafrost*: "Once You Name It"; *Ploughshares*: "Strong Stars", "Young Boy Dancing at Playa Los Muertos"; *poetryALASKAwomen: top of the world*: "Three Notes from a Wooden Flute"; *Polar Star*: Translation into Russian of "Once You Name It."

Many poems from this section were included in *Braided River*, a letterpress chapbook. Deep gratitude to Wendy Shaft (for her artwork especially) and Don Bixler of Limner Press.

from Underground Rivers

Red Hen Press, 2002

Amicus Journal: "Ajo Lily"; *Blackbird*: "Night-Blooming Jasmine"; *Looking North: Art from the University of Alaska Museum* anthology: "The Story of Light," "What to Count On," "What Will Remain"; *Nimrod International Journal of Prose and Poetry*: "What Will Remain" (titled "Wingspan of Sand"); *Prairie Schooner*: "Aubade: Morning Aurora," "Bear Plan, Brooks Range," "Hillclimb"; *Puerto del Sol*: "Too Soon after Rain"; *Steam Ticket*: "Owls' Cough Balls"; *Third Coast*: "What to Count On"; *Weber Studies*: "Pantano Wash"; *West Branch*: "Easter, Grave Tending."

"What to Count On" was posted as an example of "proof by contradiction" on a site devoted to poetry with mathematics: www.poetrywithmathematics.blogspot.com/2016/06/a-poem-contradiction.html.

A dozen of the poems from 1974 to 2005 were included in a chapbook called *Peggy Shumaker: Greatest Hits*. Thanks to Jennifer Bosveld and Pudding House Publications.

from Blaze

Red Hen Press, 2005

American Poetry Review: "Wide Icy River"; *Crab Orchard Review*: "Just This Once"; *The Nebraska Review*: "Matisse's Antoinette."

from Gnawed Bones

Red Hen Press, 2010

Alaska Quarterly Review, 30th Anniversary Issue, Poetry Feature edited by Jane Hirshfield: "Long Before We Got Here, Long After We're Gone"; *American Poetry Review*: "Chatanika"; *Blackbird*: "Deliverance," "Kus-sun-ar"; *Copper Nickel*: "Long Before We Got Here, Long After We're Gone"; *Crab Orchard Review*: "Nests, an Elegy"; *Crazyhorse*: "Land Fraud Nosebleed"; *The Gettysburg Review*: "Ha Ha Ha," "No Sign"; *International Journal of Healthcare and Humanities*: "Gnawed Bones," "No Sign"; *The Iowa Review*: "Oatmeal"; *Poetry Kantu* (Japan): "When Ground Cannot Take in More Rain"; *Prairie Schooner*: "Desert Odyssey," "Touch and Go," "In Praise, Ephemera"; *The Seattle Review*: "Naming What We Hold in Our Hands";

Thanal Online: "Beyond Words, This Language"; *Verse Daily* monthly feature: "Deliverance"; *Weber Studies*: "Mother Tongue."

"As War Goes On" is part of a letterpress broadside made by Karla Elling, printed on "combat paper" made from their uniforms by young veterans of the wars in Iraq and Afghanistan. I'm grateful to everyone involved.

"Oatmeal" was included in *Poetry Daily Essentials 2007*, edited by Diane Boller and Don Selby, and in the Seren anthology *Women's Work*, edited by Amy Wack and Eva Salzman.

A letterpress broadside printed by Heather Neal Kasvinsky features "Long Before We Got Here, Long After We're Gone" and the painting *Bright Tracks* by Kesler Woodward (2009 Alaska Arts and Culture Conference).

"In Praise, Ephemera" was exhibited at the Chicago Cultural Center along with artwork by Laura Cloud as part of the Poetic Dialogue Project.

from Toucan Nest

Red Hen Press, 2013

Pura vida and many thanks to Eloise Klein Healy, poet guide, and to Colleen Rooney, naturalist. Your invitation led to our shared trip to Costa Rica. Your knowledge and generosity made this book possible.

Thank you to our hiking, birding, and writing companions in Costa Rica—Nan Cano, Karen Kuester, Regina Lark, Mary Lintula, Rebecca Morse, Maureen O'Connell, Sue Pope, Ronni Sanlo, Georjean Seeliger, Jim Thiele, and Joe Usibelli.

Thank you to our skilled guides, Ramón Valdez and Juan Carlos Rodriguez.

Alaska Quarterly Review: "Genesis, Quetzal," "Strangler Fig," "Tent Revival"; *Clover: A Literary Rag*: "Ancestor," "How the Motmot Got That Tail"; *The Fiddlehead*: "Sloth"; *Fire on Her Tongue: An Anthology of Contemporary Women's Poetry*: "Basilisk Lizard," "Venom"; *The Gettysburg Review*: "Toucan Nest"; *Hobble Creek Review*: "Blue-Gray Tanager, Here, Gone"; *The Los Angeles Review*: "Passion Flower"; *Prairie Schooner*: "Getting Away," "Painted Cart with No Oxen"; *A River & Sound Review*: "Blue Morpho"; *Verse Wisconsin*: "Spirit of the Bat."

The American Life in Poetry syndicated newspaper column featured "Spirit of the Bat." Many thanks to Ted Kooser and Pat Emile.

Fine printer Karla Elling of Mummy Mountain Press combined her artwork with "Blue Morpho" on a magnificent and colorful letterpress broadside.

from Just Breathe Normally

University of Nebraska Press, 2007

Passages from *Just Breathe Normally* are used with permission of the University of Nebraska Press. Thank you!

Thank you to Judith Kitchen and Dawn Marano for help with this book.

Several poems from earlier books appear translated into prose in *Just Breathe Normally.* In this book you can see "The Apple" as a syllabic, lined poem and as a very brief passage of prose. "Naming What We Hold in Our Hands" appears as a lined poem and is included with more context in the prose passage "Dr. Martino."

"Moving Water, Tucson" opened the anthology *Short Takes: Brief Encounters with Contemporary Nonfiction,* edited by Judith Kitchen.

American Poetry Review: "Wilderness"; *Ascent*: "Shower"; *James River Review*: "'Mother's First Words after the Birth'"; *Trappings: Stories of Women, Power, and Clothing,* edited by Tiffany Ludwig and Renee Piechocki: "Turquoise Dress"; *Under Northern Lights,* edited by Frank Soos and Kesler Woodward: "Locket."

GRATITUDE

I'm grateful to the editors and publishers who showed hospitality to my work.

I'm grateful to the Rasmuson Foundation for its Distinguished Artist Award, which supported the completion of this book. Special thanks to Diane Kaplan and Jayson Smart.

Thank you to Artsmith, especially Jill Johnson and Charles Toxey at Kangaroo House, for a residency on Orcas Island as the Artsmith Artist of the year.

Thank you to the Alaska Humanities Forum, especially Christina Barber, curator, and Nina Kemppel, then director, for hosting the exhibition of *Sparks: A Conversation in Poems and Paintings*. Amazing thanks to Kesler Woodward for this collaboration. I'm grateful to Dorli McWayne, Joe Usibelli, Susanna Mishler. Thank you to Theresa Bakker for recording our conversation and to Robert Hannon for creating podcasts. Special thanks to Ron Spatz for publishing this whole project in *Alaska Quarterly Review* and for putting it online at www.aqreview.org/special-feature-sparks-a-conversation-in-poems-and-paintings.

Thank you to my teachers, so many, so generous.

Thank you to the booksellers who put fine work into my hands, and who held out my books to others. Special thanks to Pinna Joseph at Changing Hands and to Sue Post, Lee Post, and Jenny Stroyeck at Homer Bookstore.

Thank you to the book editors who said yes: Thomas Rabbitt at University of Alabama, Ed Ochester at the University of Pittsburgh, Ladette Randolph (previously) at University of Nebraska Press, Kate Gale and Mark Cull at Red Hen Press.

Thanks to Amy Meissner, whose art graces the cover of this book.

Thank you to Kevin Clark for his wise introduction to this collection.

Thank you to meticulous copyeditor/proofreader Joeth Zucco.

I honor and thank Adrian Koesters and Erin Hollowell for their wise advice in winnowing.

Maurya Simon, sister poet, thank you—your care and insight let me see these poems anew.

Thank you, Tito Ríos, old friend. No abstraction is worth the trouble.

Thank you to Brenda Miller for the great pleasure of writing together, and for swimming with me among hundreds of dolphins.

Thank you to Joy Harjo for her poems and for the gift of her presence at the class Eva Saulitis and I taught at the Old Japanese School near Volcano.

Thanks to Linda Hogan, who wrote to the moss.

I thank my students and colleagues over the decades—at University of Arizona, Arizona State, Old Dominion, Bucknell University, University of Alaska Fairbanks.

Special thanks to Frank Soos and John Morgan, compadres.

I thank and honor my colleagues, friends, students, and alumni of the Rainier Writing Workshop MFA at Pacific Lutheran University.

To all my writer friends over all the years and all the miles, I'm grateful.

Special thanks to Naomi Shihab Nye, Hilda Raz, Jane Hirshfield, Christianne Balk, Toi Derricotte, Alicia Ostriker, Mark Spragg, Cynthia Hogue, Karla Elling, Al Young, Carole Oles, Sherry Simpson, Jennifer Brice, Ernestine Hayes, Alison Hawthorne Deming, Stan Rubin, Katharine Coles, Norman Dubie, Rachel Rose, Dinty Moore, Camille Dungy, Oliver de la Paz, Aldona Jonaitis, Natalie Diaz, Forrest Gander, Debbie Moderow, Kate Carroll de Gutes, David Lee, Wendy Barker, Marvin Bell, Kevin Clark, Fleda Brown, Rebecca McClanahan, Rick Barot, David Huddle, Sherwin Bitsui, Rita Dove, David Biespiel, Lupita Barron-Ríos, Lia Purpura, Greg Glazner, Linda Bierds, Kevin Goodan, Suzanne Berne, Barrie Jean Borich, David Allen Cates, Rigoberto Gonzalez, Adrianne Harun, Jim Heynen, Jenny Johnson, Dinah Lenney, Kent Meyers, Scott Nadelson, Ann Pancake, Marjorie Sandor, Julie Marie Wade . . .

Eva Saulitis, Lucille Clifton, Judith Kitchen, Maxine Kumin, William Kloefkorn, Judith Ortiz Cofer, Derick Burleson, Seamus Heaney, C. D. Wright, Eduardo Galeano, your spirits entwine. I miss you.

Thank you to Craig Matkin, Mara Liebling, and all of Eva Saulitis's loving family and friends.

Deepest gratitude to Kesler Woodward for our many collaborations, especially our yearlong artistic conversation and our many-years-long friendship.

Book artist Margo Klass has spent untold hours in her studio binding each of my books by hand, selecting distinctive and beautiful wood to shape into covers, which she completed with found objects. I'm overwhelmed and honored by her art, and completely grateful. (For two years she kept this secret. My husband started this, her husband Frank Soos knew, Kes Woodward knew, Dorli McWayne knew, my brother and his wife knew, John Manthei knew. I had no clue. How did they manage that?)

Thank you to Carol Swartz for allowing me to be part of the Kachemak Bay Writers' Conference.

Thank you to everyone who's been part of the Fairbanks Summer Arts Festival Creative Writing class over the years, especially Jeanne Clark. Writing with you has been a privilege.

Thank you to everyone at the Alaska State Council on the Arts and the Alaska Arts & Culture Foundation. You enrich our lives.

Thank you to the National Endowment for the Arts for a long-ago fellowship in poetry that came at a crucial time.

Dancing thanks to the crew at Red Hen Press, especially Kate Gale, editor and friend, and Mark Cull, man of magnificent imagination. Thanks to Tobi Harper, Selena Trager, Alisa Trager, Keaton Maddox, and Hannah Moye.

Thank you to my siblings, Ginny, Sue, John & Pam—you sustain me. Thank you to the next generations: Hanna & Beej, Nico, Mateo; Hillary & Jesse; Daniel & Kalila, Julian; Hope, Viktor; Amy & Dave, Amaya, Asher; Melanie, Malik, Desia, Lukas. Thanks to the Moen cousins and the Langley cousins.

Thank you to the Usibelli clan: Joe, Marilyn, Lexi; Cathy, Trevor, Tara, Jesse; Mitch, Michele, Nathan, Jackie, Lina; Anna, Ted, Micah, Marissa, Owen; Rob; Sean. Thanks to Rosie & George, Rick, Roz, Shelley, Julia, and their families.

Ever and always, thanks beyond measure to Joe.

Photo credit: Todd Paris

PEGGY SHUMAKER is the daughter of two deserts—the Sonoran Desert where she grew up and the subarctic desert of interior Alaska where she lives now. Shumaker was honored by the Rasmuson Foundation as its Distinguished Artist. She served as Alaska State Writer Laureate. She received a poetry fellowship from the National Endowment for the Arts. Shumaker is the author of eight books of poetry, including *Cairn*, her new and selected volume. Her lyrical memoir is *Just Breathe Normally*. Professor emerita from University of Alaska Fairbanks, Shumaker teaches in the Rainier Writing Workshop MFA at Pacific Lutheran University. She serves on the advisory board for Storyknife and on the board of the Alaska Arts and Culture Foundation. Shumaker is editor of the Boreal Books series (an imprint of Red Hen Press), editor of the Alaska Literary Series at University of Alaska Press, poetry editor of *Persimmon Tree*, and contributing editor for *Alaska Quarterly Review*. Please visit her website at www.peggyshumaker.com.